A Gestalt Theory of the Universe and the Mind

A Gestalt Theory of the Universe and the Mind

SENTIO, ERGO SUM!

結搭宇宙心靈說

Tainan Lee 李清木

© 2022 by Tainan Lee

All rights reserved. This book or any portion thereof may not be reproduced or used in any manner whatsoever without the express written permission of the publisher except for the use of brief quotations in a book review.

ISBN: 979-8-9852115-1-1 (paperback)

Contents

Overview vii
Section I 1
The Universe of Yin-Yang Strands
A Gestalt Theory of Creation, Gravity, Relativity, Spacetime
陰陽結搭宇宙說

Section II 57
The Mind Gestalts
A Gestalt Theory of their Formation and Function
結搭心靈說

摘要 (Abstract in Traditional Chinese) 103
About the Author and the Book by Ytenne Lee 107

Overview

The Void. Since before the Beginning, there has always been the Void, which has neither dimension nor time, energy, or matter. It now houses our Universe and other universes, if any. The portion of the Void that our Universe occupies we call the Space. In the Space, traversed voids still exist everywhere, such as inside the atom and between galaxies.

The Creation. A single point in the Void is not definable for lack of location, time, quantity, and dimension. It takes two points surviving together in the Void to start a Creation, for then there is a line with a changeable distance-time. Further, three points make a surface, and four points complete a 3-D reference system, thereby converting distance-time to space-time. That is to say, the gestaltation of points makes something out of nothing. The Universe could therefore be created by a yin-yang gestalt that self-perpetuated.

Yin and yang are *nonbeing* and sum to nothing.

Tainan Lee 李清木

However, their zero-sum multiplication, being costless, became unstoppable. The pre-Universe of yins and yangs then grew to saturation, exploded at the Big Bang, and shredded to become strands. A strand has a yin-yang core, yin endings, and yang endings that impart gravity and activity. Freestanding strands and their small gestalts now form the Sea of Strands that holds the Universe, frames the space-time, cradles the galaxies, and relays electromagnetic energy transport. Strands further gestaltate to become photons, subatomic particles, particles, and the dark energy-matter. Larger gestalts (of gestalts) form energy-matter including the atoms, the molecules, the stars, and the galaxies. Time was not independently created. It only marks the changes of things. It started as pre-time with yin 1 and yang 1. Pre-time became time upon the Big Bang.

The Universe of gestalts. The Universe is a gestalt; so is everything in it. Energy, matter, things, and the human mind are all gestalts. A military maneuver and an organic stereochemical structure are good examples of the power of gestaltation. Gestalts can be relatively stable or very transient. The sun has a stable gestalt of matter, while it radiates transient gestalts of energies. Gestaltation creates gestalts that end with re-gestaltation. Every activity in the Universe is an act of gestaltation. A clock is a recurrent gestalt that marks time, seen when subatomic particles oscillate, pendulums swing, Earth spins and spirals, and galaxies swirl. Nothing is permanent.

A gestalt has something not found in its components

or their sum. The nucleus and the electrons are not the atoms; their gestalt is.

Likewise, water molecules make the oceans, the sunsets, the waves, and the icebergs by gestaltation. However, as yins and yangs are *nonbeing*, their gestalts are practically *empty and inconstant*, including the strands, the atoms, and the galaxies.

The mind gestalts. The neurons gestaltate strategically to make efficient gestalts of synapses. Gestalts of synapses, in turn, generate gestalts of action potentials that form mind gestalts. The neuronal and synaptic gestalts are relatively stable, while the electromagnetic mind gestalts are fleeting.

Gestalts are real when recognized by mind gestalts. All sentients have sentience gestalts that enable them to sense, to recognize, to act, as well as to enjoy and to suffer. Higher sentients also have the "I" gestalts that recognize self and others. They further develop intelligence, wisdom, religion, and culture. When we pray, we send, via the Sea of Strands, devout mind gestalts entreating to be heard by our deity in the Space-Time Web.

The gestalt theory. A gestalt theory can be developed that the Universe was created out of nothing and continues to sum to nothing, but everything we know is something real and dear to us as a gestalt. In parallel analogy, the gestaltation of yins and yangs created the pre-Universe, and the gestaltation of the yin strands and yang strands created the Universe. Further, gestalts of the synaptic action potentials of the cortical neurons constitute the mind. The gestalt theory ventures to offer a unified view of *being* and *nonbeing,* the *wave* and *particle* duality of photons, as well as the *Universe* (Section I) and the *mind* (Section II).

Cogito, ergo sum? Am I real? "I think; therefore, I am?" Even the realness of "I" has been fundamentally questioned. Nevertheless, everything is real to us as a gestalt, especially when recognized by the "I" gestalt. *Sentio, ergo sum.* Being sentient, I am!

A Gestalt Theory of the Universe and the Mind

SENTIO, ERGO SUM!

結搭宇宙心靈說

Tainan Lee 李清木

Section I: The Universe of Yin-Yang Strands

Section I
The Universe of Yin-Yang Strands
A Gestalt Theory of Creation, Gravity, Relativity, Spacetime
陰陽結搭宇宙說
Abstract (Section 1)......................... 1
Theory...................................... 5
Preamble
The Sub-infinitesimal Binary Creation
The Unstoppable Zero-Sum Multiplication
The Explosion and the Strands
The Transition from Pre-Universe to Universe
The Loss of Constants and the Evolution of Dimensions
The Particles, Energy, Matter, Celestial Bodies
The Physics of Small Gestalts, The Quanta
The Void, the Traversed Voids, the Local Voids
The Finite Universe

Tainan Lee 李清木

The Sea of Strands as Infrastructure of the Universe
The Variable Space-Time Curvatures
The forever Variability and Changeability
The Fate of the Universe
Discussion **23**
One Universe, Lowest Cost of Creation
The Creation, The Yin-Yang 凹凸 Gestalt
Quantity Mathematics of the Universe
Gestalt Dynamics
No Straight Line, Level Plane, True Circle, Symmetry
Spacetime Curves, Light Beams, Particles, Photons
Variable Time, Clock, Light-Year, E/M Ratio
Dating the Universe and Locating Remote
    Galaxies: A Long View.
The Swirling Universe and Subverses
Domino Chain Reactions, Traveling Cosmic Lights
Atomic Electrons, Hopping Spiraling Photons,
    Hopping Time
Beyond Sciences, Philosophy **43**
Our Subverse: Its Past, its Present, its Mysteries
Emptiness, Inconstancy, Conservation of Strands
Humanity, Mind, Feng Shui, Yin-Yang Culture
The Extraterrestrials and our Space Neighborhood
Save Our Planet Earth

Abstract

IN PHYSICS, CREATING SOMETHING OUT of nothing is impossible. Because of this, it is no paradox that the Universe itself must have come from nothing, or there would be nothing and no Universe. In the Void, originally there was no space-time, no energy-matter, and no dimensions. How could anything ever come about? First, yin 1 appeared, and, before there was time, it induced yang 1 in order to pay the cost and restore nothingness. However, non-simultaneity and nonsymmetric mobility prevented yang 1 from canceling out yin 1. This necessitated yin 1 to induce yang 2 in a second self-balancing act to restore nothingness. This further necessitated yang 1 to likewise induce yin 2. Once their mutual cancellation was avoided, yins and yangs repeated their mutual inductions unstoppably. Ad infinitum, in every unit of *pre-time*, every yin of every generation, old and young, induced a yang, while every yang likewise induced a yin. Generations of alternating yins and yangs formed branching yin-yang strings, while every yin surrounded herself with sons, and every yang surrounded himself with daughters. Needing no input, the *zero-sum multiplication* encountered no limit and proceeded in extreme geometric progression throughout the pre-time. Then, at Time Zero, the Ball saturated at the center, reached singular density, and exploded, triggered by the breakage of a yin-yang bond. In chain reactions, the entire Ball of the pre-Universe broke into *strands*. During the Bang, yins and yangs continued to procreate and to saturate, until the Explosion finished when the pre-Universe became the primitive Universe.

Each strand has a core of yin-yang string and branches with yin endings or yang endings. The unmatched endings impart polarity, gravity, and reactivity. The vibrant strands then formed energy-matter by gestaltation, including sub-particles, particles, atoms, stars, and galaxies. They also align to form the Sea of Strands.

The Sea of Strands still holds a major portion of energy-matter of the Universe in the form of freestanding strands or their small gestalts. It now fabricates the infrastructure of the Universe, provides the matrix for celestial bodies, and maintains the space-time framework. Strands and their small gestalts also mediate the travel of electromagnetic energy.

At the instant of the Bang, distance and time started together as one dimension, the *distance-time* (Dt). Time did not emerge by itself; it only marked changes of things, *firstly* of distance. Spatial dimensions of distance (width, depth, height) then followed to shape the space-time.

Space-time dimensions remain dynamic and inseparable from the underlying distance-time dimension.

The Universe is practically empty and remains a big gestalt of zero-sum. Strands and individual gestalts inside the Universe, however, do not sum to zero. They are multiform and active, and they re-gestaltate incessantly under the post-Bang laws of physics. Everything in the Universe is a gestalt. Photons and particles are small quantal gestalts of strands. Stars and galaxies are large gestalts of gestalts; so is the entire Universe.

Photons do not travel waving or zigzagging forward in a level plane, for there is no level plane. They do not travel in a rotating plane, either, because nothing makes them cross the center of the plane in every cycle. They spiral forward, hopping in narrow tubal paths, *strand to strand*. A hopping, spiraling photon is detectable as a particle and a wave but not as both simultaneously. The Universe has no straight line, level plane, perfect circle, or real symmetry. The path of light follows the space-time curves formed by lines of strands. It is considered straight only for convenience by the *Homo sapiens*.

Buddha recognized the emptiness and inconstancy of things in the Universe. René Descartes accepted "Cogito, ergo sum." True to both nothingness and the ergo *sum*, everything *is* real as a gestalt.

This includes the yin-yang duos, all forms of energy-matter, and the mind gestalts that enable all sentients to recognize self and realness. This author says, "*Sentio*, ergo sum!" *Being sentient, I am.* Mind gestalts also enable sentients to enjoy and to suffer.

Should a yin-yang duo be squeezed into one same space-time, they both will vanish. Should a chain annihilation ensue, the Universe will diminish. Should a lone yin or lone yang survive unhindered in the refreshed Void, a zero-sum multiplication Act II might follow to start a universe anew. As a life lasts a *lifetime*, a universe will last a *universe time*—no more, no less.

Theory

Preamble

It is popular nowadays to say that our Universe began with a Big Bang. But *what was there to bang*? Prior to the existence of anything to bang, the Universe must start with nothing, for anything supposed to be its origin must ultimately come from nothing. Once started, the pre-Universe must grow unhindered, by very small increments, very fast, and nonstop until a major event (the Big Bang) suddenly changed it into a system of space-time and energy-matter governed by laws of physics. The creating steps must be simplistic and non-stoppable. The components must be small and counterbalanced. The process must require no external inputs and incur no deficit. Further, true to *the ultimate law of preservation*, the entire Universe must maintain a zero sum and permit a mechanism for return to nothingness. Meanwhile, everything in the Universe must be *verifiably real* to another. This preamble leads to a gestalt theory of the Universe that also explains the mind and feelings of all sentients. A gestalt is a state of verifiable realness, with parts but without energy-matter of its own.

Tainan Lee 李清木

The Sub-infinitesimal Binary Creation

To create anything out of nothing is immeasurably difficult, if not impossible. Next to impossibility, yin 1 (the first yin), of *nearo*[*] quantity or no quantity, somehow appeared in the Void. It wiggles. Upon its first move, it left behind a super void, where its complement, yang 1 (the first yang), was induced in *nearo* time, or no time. The sequentiality of their appearance and their mobility saved them from mutual cancellation. The duo then balanced each other and vibrated in sync. In gestalt, this yin-yang duo became the first *being*. Namely, yin+yang = /-1/ + /+1/ = duo, *in gestalt*, although yin+yang = (-1) + (+1) = 0, *in mathematics*. Yin and yang are two states of one same thing (or nothing), in complement to each other, not opposite each other. *Neither is a being alone.* They sum to zero but exist in duo as a gestalt.

The Unstoppable Zero-Sum Multiplication

Unannihilated, yin 1 induced yang 2 in the next nearotime, while yang 1 also induced yin 2. Repetitive counterbalancing acts ensued. Being one nearotime late, each inductee balanced out but failed to cancel out its parent. It only paved the way for another generation to ensue in the next

---

[*] It is essential to define *nearo*. For lack of a better term, it stands for "near zero," *the smallest ever*. *Nearotime* bridges no time and time. Likewise, *nearo quantity* bridges nothing and something. It is not clear how many *nearotimes* make a Planck time, which is of the order of 10^{-43} s. In general, *nearo* bridges nonbeing and being. *Nearo* is intended for the pre-Universe only. As such, it is much smaller than the post-Bang *infinitesimal*. Whereas *infinitesimal* is vague, *nearo* is a precise pre-quantity, the indivisible *(atomos)* basic measure of the pre-Universe.

nearotime. It further reduced the risk of mutual annihilation. The multiplication was destined to repeat *nonstop*.

Ergo, in every nearotime, every yin of every generation induced a son yang, while every yang of every generation induced a daughter yin. The costless multiplication became unstoppable and proceeded with a wild geometric progression. There was unrestricted extension and branching of strings after strings. All along, however, the entire pre-Universe remained balanced, with a zero-sum.

The growing Ball attained the singular density but remained small, as yins and yangs of *nearo* size packed with no spacing. Nothing in the post-Bang Universe can fathom the density of the Ball. As each step occurred so fast, the unlimited multiplication did not take long in the post-Bang timescale to reach a breaking point. The surface of the Ball should remain even and round all along, with about the same numbers of yins and yangs at the surface and throughout.

Figure: NASA photo of the sun, taken to illustrate the saturating Ball ready to explode

Tainan Lee 李清木

THE EXPLOSION AND THE STRANDS

As the Ball grew, packed with absolute density, branching, crowding, and stretching increased focal vulnerability. However, even when yin 1 became saturated, she still had to induce the next yang to maintain equilibrium. Further, in every nearotime, one next generation of yins and yangs would reach saturation. Explosion was the only possible outcome. The yin 1–yang 1 bond, being the most loaded, would be the first to break. The uniform composition of the Ball and the quick succession of saturating generations of yins and yangs should assure a fast, thorough, even, and violent explosion, generally called the Big Bang.

The Ball eventually broke into strands. Strands are similar but may have quite a few varieties. They are the indivisible (*atomos*) building blocks of everything in the Universe. Each strand consists of a core string of yins and yangs, with branches of variable lengths.

Strands are likely longer than wide (oblong), with yin endings and yang endings that impart polarity, gravity, and reactivity. They are asymmetrical, polar along the core, and yin or yang as a whole and at the branches.

Stillness is not an option. The yins and yangs wiggle, likely once every nearotime. Strands also wiggle and twist around their cores. The rhythmicity of the yin-yang duos permeated the entire pre-Universe. Likewise, the rhythmicity of the dancing strands permeates the entire Universe. This sets the fundamental rhythmicity of the Universe. The relationship between the rhythmicity of the yin-yang duos of the pre-Universe and the rhythmicity of the strands of the Universe is unknown. Somehow, their rhythmicity should also underlie the vibration of the particles and the atoms, so that the Universe has a coordinated rhythmicity.

The strands attract, align, and resonate with one another. They interact, gestaltate, and re-gestaltate incessantly. Some strands gestaltate to form energy-matter, but most remain freestanding.

As one whole gestalt, the Sea of Strands (of free strands and their small gestalts) provides the matrix, fabricates the infrastructure, mediates transport of electromagnetic energy, and maintains the space-time framework for the ensuing Universe. See discussion.

THE TRANSITION FROM PRE-UNIVERSE TO UNIVERSE

From the Beginning to the completion of the Explosion, during a brief transition from pre-time to time, the pre-Universe transformed into the neonatal Universe. During this transition, younger generations of yins and yangs in the outgoing pieces continued to procreate and to saturate one generation every nearotime. As a result, the ensuing Universe is likely very much more massive than the Ball. See also "Quantity Mathematics of the Universe" below.

The first pieces of the exploding Ball shot into the true Void, encountering no impedance. The continued growth and explosion of the outgoing pieces (sub-Bangs) compounded the Bang dynamics. While some sub-sub-pieces shot forward, others shot sideways and backward. Therefore, the ensuing Universe is *generally* a filled sphere, not hollow like a soccer ball or a balloon.

During the transition, the newborn Universe was a mixture of chunks of the broken Ball and newly formed strands in varying proportions. By the time the explosion was complete, the Universe already had congregated strands undergoing gestaltation to form atoms and stars. The physics of the transitional Universe is beyond comprehension. Upon completion of the Bang, Creation stopped, while expansion continued. The center of the Universe should remain where it was, although the Void offers no reference for us to locate where it is. We can never see the other half Universe from our half Universe. One can surmise that the strands and the Universe have a bias pointing toward its center because of gravity. There is more on this in the discussion.

THE LOSS OF CONSTANTS AND THE EVOLUTION OF DIMENSIONS

In the Ball, each yin-yang induction occurred in one discrete quantal unit of pre-time, a nearotime. Conceivably, yins and yangs continue their dance inside the strands, post-Bang. Other constants of the pre-Universe are lost forever, including the time from yin 1 to the Bang, the size and density of the Ball at the Bang, and the initial speed of the outgoing pieces at the Bang. Post-Bang, there is no constancy, and the mobile variform strands constantly gestaltate and re-gestaltate. Exceptions may be that the rhythmicity of the strands is constant, and the zero-sum of the Universe remains true. The zero-sum should hold true even in the scenario of yin-yang annihilation; see "The Fate of the Universe."

As pieces of the Ball shot out, one dimension appeared: the distance. Distance is obligatorily coupled with time, so that the distance-time, D_t, is the only primary independent dimension of the Universe. As pieces of the Ball and then the strands moved out in every direction, the spatial dimensions (x, y, z) ensued. So did their angular addresses from the center of the Universe and from one another. All spatial dimensions are relative, with no fixed reference point, and all are obligatorily tied to time. Time was not independently created. It only times changes. It times the changing distance-time and then the changing space-time. As the space-time curves and light travels the curvy space-time, light's speed and direction also become relative. Ultimately, physics means how strands gestalt and re-gestaltate *over time,* in energy-matter and in space-time.

The Particles, Energy, Matter, Celestial Bodies

The Bang converted singularity into multiplicity in a time span too short to fathom precisely with the post-Bang timescale. The force was also unfathomable. Post-Bang, strands continually gestaltate and re-gestaltate. As small as subatomic particles and as large as the galaxies, all forms of energy-matter are gestalts of strands or gestalts of gestalts. The Universe in toto still sums to zero and thus remains nonexistent to other universes, *if any*. However, each strand does not have a zero net. Their gestalts do not sum to zero either. They are real. See Section II.

Most strands and their small gestalts are freestanding, and they form the Sea of Strands (*v.i.*). With time, some relatively mobile gestalts of strands take on the features of energy, and they may further gestaltate to become matter. Conversely, relatively stable gestalts take on the features of matter, but they may emit particles to shoot away as energy. *As alternative gestaltations of strands, energy and matter are interchangeable.* The exchange rate between energy and matter, as figured out by scientists on planet Earth, is $E=mc^2$, wherein the speed of light, c, is taken as a constant. See more in "Variable Time, Space-Time Curves" in the discussion.

Not only may energy and matter interchange, but energy particles and strands may also interchange. Further, strands may diminish by yin-yang annihilation. See "The Fate of the Universe" below and "Conservation of Strands" in the discussion.

THE PHYSICS OF SMALL GESTALTS, THE QUANTA

On a small scale, a few strands may gestaltate to form a small physical entity, such as a sub-particle, a particle, a quantum, or a photon. In reverse, these small particles may lose strands and degrade. They may also disintegrate to revert to free strands, and thus "vanish" into the Sea of Strands. This would be at odds with the present-day laws of conservation of energy-matter. See "Emptiness, Inconstancy, and Conservation of Strands" in the discussion. As strands gestaltate, de-gestaltate, and re-gestaltate in and out of physical status, the small particles will be unstable, elusive, and hard to assay. They may jump around unpredictably, for there could be little or nothing between their successive locations. The way they jump and bounce reflects some quantal inter-strand distances around them and should vary with the local sea of strands they are in. The physics of small gestalts of strands is quantal.

THE VOID, THE TRAVERSED VOIDS, THE LOCAL VOIDS

The true Void has no dimension, no address, and no system of reference. With the Bang, the strands dispersed to occupy a part of the Void that we call our Space. Relative to the size of the Ball, the Universe is immeasurably huge. And the Space is practically empty. Inside, local spaces are defined by their occupants.

Even when they exist as matter, all gestalts are mostly empty. As the electrons gestaltate with the nucleus, the resulting atom remains mostly empty. Likewise, larger gestalts such as our solar system and the galaxies are practically empty.

Unlike the true Void, intra-Universe voids are populated by strands and their small gestalts, framed by space-time, pervaded by gravity, and traveled by electromagnetic energies. In other words, voids in the Universe are qualified. Intra-atomic voids, galactic voids, and intergalactic voids differ. Energy particles may travel various voids differently, depending on the local sea of strands and space-time.

THE FINITE UNIVERSE

The yins and yangs inside the Ball had pre-physics and pre-dimensions. They had pre-time, pre-distance, pre-energy and pre-gravity in minute primordial quantal units. Yins and yangs are too small, too many, and too fast to fathom with post-Bang physics. As each yin-yang induction took a tiny nearotime, it would take an unfathomably long pre-time for the tiny yins and yangs to grow the Ball to the size that contained the pre-Universe. However, the Ball must be very small and very short-lived in post-Bang scales. It built up tremendous explosive power as yins and yangs packed tight and multiplied extremely fast in a process that allowed no time, no room and *no way* for decompression. It is no paradox that the Ball became great by accumulation of *nearo* smallness in fast nearotime steps.

Upon completion of the Bang, everything became separately surrounded by a local void. Creation stopped, pre-time became time, and the Universe became finite.

As re-Creation succeeded Creation, everything must come from something else, according to the laws of physics. Except for a nearotime when yin 1 was alone, the sum total of the pre-Universe was zero, and the sum total of the Universe remains zero. By analogy, the gestaltation of yins and yangs created the pre-Universe; the gestaltation of yin strands and yang strands formed the Universe.

THE SEA OF STRANDS AS INFRASTRUCTURE OF THE UNIVERSE

Strands are freestanding except those in energy-matter gestalts. The unbound strands and their small gestalts account for a major portion of the Universe. They might include the dark energy-matter. As one gestalt, the Sea of Strands fabricates the infrastructure of the Universe and frames the space-time. It is the matrix of the Universe. This is somewhat akin to how water molecules cradle everything that water holds in the sea, shape the sea, and relay wave energy (pressure energy) of water in the sea.

The strands dance back and forth, marking time in rhythmicity that could relate to the dance of the yin-yang duo. The rhythmicity of the Sea of Strands is the basic rhythmicity of the Universe. It could be related to the Planck time. The strands also align in various local patterns while maintaining a bias toward gravity. Therefore, while the strands of the Universe as a whole point to the center of the Universe, local strands point mainly to local foci of gravity. This is akin to how apples fall to the ground, while Earth and everything around the sun (including apples) gravitate toward the sun.

Local seas of strands mediate local gravitational and electromagnetic fields. Via the surrounding strands, the sun, Earth, the moon, and the apples maintain blended, dynamic, and balanced gravitational fields. Likewise, Earth, the magnet, and the iron sands maintain blended, balanced magnetic fields. One is tempted to speculate that the orientation of the strands also underlies the perpendicular relationship (the right-hand law) among the electrical current, the magnetic field, and the moving conductor.

The gravity of common objects on Earth has been well exploited. Gravitational forces and paths of celestial bodies in the solar system have been measured precisely enough to enable scientists to send *Perseverance* to Mars. However, gravity-mass relationships between solar systems and among the constellations are hard to define in kilogram terms. With distances of billions of light-years, their masses can hardly be imagined to generate sufficient gravity to keep the Universe in one piece and in order, without the Sea of Strands as an infrastructural cradle.

The Sea of Strands also transport electromagnetic energy. That is how electromagnetic energy passes through voids and vacuums but not beyond the Universe. With some similarity, molecules of air and water relay sound and pressure, copper atoms relay electricity, and strands and their small gestalts relay the electromagnetic energies, including the travel of light.

The strands in a relay can be likened to the steel balls in the Newton's cradle. When the inciting ball hits the chain, the energy is transmitted instantly to the other end ball, which swings out. All other balls vibrate in situ. A Newton's cradle is a lineal model. It can have variable number of steel balls. Its transmission depends mainly on how the balls transmit the impact. The strands dancing in situ are the extreme relayers for light particles, making light the fastest and farthest-reaching traveler in the Universe. Nonetheless, the travel of light is limited and dependent on strands and varies with local space-time. Sounds of all pitches travel in air at one speed; electromagnetic energies of all frequencies likewise travel the Sea of Strands at one speed. Both are medium-dependent, subject to local conditions and the Doppler effect. See the "Space-Time Curves" and "Atomic Photons" sections in the discussion.

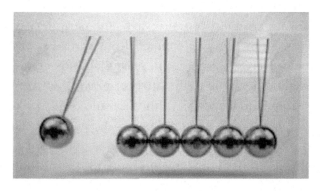

Figure: A Newton's cradle

Tainan Lee 李清木

For lack of medium, we cannot send test beams beyond our Universe to study the Void or other universes, if any. Besides, any probe we send will be pulled back by gravity. The Universe is not losing weight when stars explode, because the Sea of Strands hold all electromagnetic energies within. We cannot send a test beam to study the other hemi-Universe either. Near the center and the periphery of the Universe, and around major gravity foci, lights likely travel differently from how we normally see them here on Earth.

THE VARIABLE SPACE-TIME CURVATURES

As a whole, the Sea of Strands defines the Space and contains the Universe. The strands themselves are held together by their innate yin-yang attraction. They are not in contiguity. By analogy, water molecules in the aquatic seas are held together by their intermolecular forces. However, liquid H_2O molecules are contiguous, because they are bulky, weighted down, and less energetic.

Local densities of strands vary. The periphery of the Universe must be a vast zone of thinly spread strands of eternal peace. Elsewhere, the seas of strands cradle the celestial bodies. Due to the intrinsic gravity between yins and yangs and between strands, strands will surround heavier stars with higher density. As stars in galaxies whirl, the seas of strands will manifest local "weather," with local variations in concentration, pressure, and flow. There will be waves, eddies, and whirlpools of strands three-dimensionally.

Water molecules gestaltate to make bodies of water. A ball immersed in a body of water curves the gestaltation lines of water molecules around it. Water flowing around the ball will change speed, direction, and pressure and curve around. In analogy, strands gestaltate to make seas of strands. Celestial bodies, or any physical body such as an apple, will likewise curve the gestaltation lines of the strands around them. Electromagnetic energy traveling by them will likewise change speed and direction and curve around.

A moving body in a sea of strands compresses the strands in its front and thins them in its wake. This is comparable to a moving object in the atmosphere or in water compressing the air or water molecules in its front and thinning them in its wake. Fast-swirling galaxies with big whirling stars likely create big wakes of scanty strands. Toward the periphery of the Universe, such wakes of rarefaction may interdigitate with gulfs of the true Void. There, in the protruding peninsulas of the Universe, physics may exhibit asymmetry, with gravity biasing toward the Universe along the spiral arms. For lack of strands between them, the "nearby" peninsulas are likely *far apart*, with no direct passage for light beams.

Each line in the space-time curvature consists of *a line of strands*. Along these space-time lines, electromagnetic particles would hop from strand to strand. The space-time curves are four-dimensional, but contemporaneous physical bodies immersed in a sea of strands together will relate to each other mainly three-dimensionally. This is akin to how water pressure passes along lines of water molecules and how a fish feels the dynamics of the sea water around them. Unlike the seas of strands, aquatic seas of planet Earth are particularly subject to the gravity of Earth, resulting in surface swells, waves, and ripples. See also "The Sea of Strands" above and "The Gestalts in the Space-Time Web" in Section II.

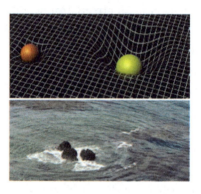

Figure. One-layer still renderings of curved space-time lines; an ESA photo illustrating space-time curves around two gravitational bodies, *upper;* a surface view of seawater curved by rocks, *lower*

THE FOREVER VARIABILITY AND CHANGEABILITY
Strands are multiform and active. Gestaltations further increase variability and changeability. Everything in the Universe is unique and changes with the local space-time it is in. Even voids vary.

Every gestalt is subject to re-gestaltation. Nothing stands still. Nothing can be exactly retraced. Ultimately, if distance is measured by the number of strands covered, the speed of light will vary with the local sea of strands. It can be nearly "constant" only where strands are relatively evenly spread. Where there are no strands, there will be no light beams. See also "Spacetime Curves" in the discussion.

THE FATE OF THE UNIVERSE

Along the whirling spirals, the crooked billion-year-old light beams can hardly tell us whether the Universe is expanding, and if so, which way and how fast. See also "Whirling and Dominoes" in the discussion section. We can neither surmise if or when the Universe will stop expanding, nor whether it will gravitate back inward in one piece.

Meanwhile, there will always be whirling, swirling, and spiraling, which tend to concentrate energy-matter toward the eddy centers. Next, the mass centers will attract one another within reach in a self-perpetuating process. Even as the periphery of the Universe thins out and local explosions shatter stars, mass centers in the Universe will gain. They will even rake in the strands from their surrounding seas of strands. After all, gravity is intrinsic to yins, yangs, and the strands. It is universal and ultimate. Eventually, it will prevail. However, we cannot tell when. We can neither guess whether it will ever reclaim strands that already spread far and thin. Meanwhile, caught between expansion and gravitation, the Universe will become ever more inhomogeneous. Galaxies and subverses will get denser while drifting farther apart.

Should a yin and her yang be ever aligned in one space-time and squeezed into each other, perhaps inside a dense blackhole, they will vanish together. Such annihilation, against the present-day laws of conservation, is possible only at the level of yins and yangs. With chain annihilation, the Universe will diminish. At an extreme, the Universe may vanish. Luckily, if one last yin or yang should survive alone in the refreshed true Void, unencumbered, it may start a new universe as yin 1 did before. Chances of yin-yang annihilation are hard to assess.

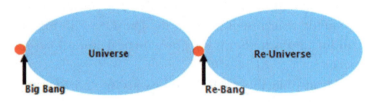

Figure: Big Bang, Universe, re-Bang, re-Universe: a timeline illustration of *two universe times*. Not to scale, *x* time, *y* size.

Discussion

ONE UNIVERSE, LOWEST COST OF CREATION
The Ball was homogeneous, and it likely exploded evenly, keeping its entire content in one Universe. Perhaps much less likely, if the yin 1–yang 1 bond broke to split the Ball into two even halves, there could be a commingling diverse or two overlapping universes.

Further, if the Ball broke into several pieces, these pieces could become various galaxies, or they could form subverses or multiverses. The scenario of a comingling diverse is interesting, considering how close yin 1 and yang 1 were to each other when the Explosion began. How our Verse (our Universe) relates to our twin verse is beyond the scope of speculation of this theory. So is the possibility that our twin verse is a "dark universe" with us.

Are there universes other than our Universe? We can never tell. Nothing can cross the true Void to bring us information. Besides, universes likely differ in their yin-yang duos and strands and may not recognize one another even side by side. As long as we think ours is the only one, or the only recognizable one, we will be happy to call it the *Uni*verse, the one and only, *unique* and *uno*.

Can the Universe be created in a different way? One alternative mechanism is for yin 1 and yang 1 to appear simultaneously. This would spare the initial awkward unbalanced solo existence of yin 1 for a nearotime. But it would predispose yin 1 and yang 1 to immediate mutual cancellation and would require every successive creative step to be a double effort.

THE CREATION, THE YIN-YANG 凹凸 GESTALT

The appearance of yin 1 is unexplainable except by Creation. But what was created then? Not a *thing*. The lone yin 1, as a solo point in the Void, was not recognizable as a being. It had no dimension and would not survive. The formation of the yin-yang duo was then the *Creation*, for it brought about dimension and reference, necessitated continued procreation, and ensured existence. All subsequent events are *re-creations* by gestaltation. Cultures and religions may recognize the *Creation* and all subsequent major re-creations as God's creations. Examples of such major re-creations include the creation of man as well as the man-woman duo.

As a yin and a yang dance together, they define a dynamic space shaped like a dumbbell or a jellybean. The duo could also be shaped like a miniature two-atom molecule of hydrogen, oxygen, or nitrogen. Although it contains no void, the tiny yin-yang gestalt is practically empty, because it is occupied only by two *nonbeings*.

A Gestalt Theory of the Universe and the Mind

Figure: Yin-yang duo as a gestalt. Yin and yang, illustrated as the small round black-and-white dots, dance in complement to make a dumbbell-shaped gestalt, *left*. The dumbbell spins to occupy a ball-shaped space, *middle*. The duo further oscillates in a larger occupied space, modeled here like a model atom, *right*. Since yin and yang individually are *nonbeing*, the gestalt is practically empty. Only in *gestalt*, the duo becomes recognizable as a *being*.

Yin and yang are the same nonbeings in gestalt (subbeing), not two opposite beings. They oscillate in complement between two states, an 凹 state and a 凸 state, namely a yin state and a yang state. (Note: 凹 reads *au*; 凸 reads *tu* in Chinese. They mean what they depict.) The yin-yang gestalt (陰陽結搭) in this theory is therefore also called the 凹凸 gestalt (凹凸結搭).

QUANTITY MATHEMATICS OF THE UNIVERSE

The zero-sum multiplication of the Ball has a theoretical limit. Yin 1 would reach her limit when she became saturated with her sons (yang 1, yang 2, yang 3…yangω) at her age of ω nearotimes.

Tainan Lee 李清木

Every other yin and yang would have one fewer spot for its children—namely, the spot already taken by its parent. However, upon the split of a saturating yin-yang bond, this vacant spot can be filled by child ω. Besides her ω number of sons, yin 1 at maturation would have ω lines of offspring varying from one to almost ω members in length. Considering that all yins and yangs would saturate one generation every nearotime, that all newborn yins and yangs of every generation would begin to procreate in one nearotime, and further that the vacated spot may be replaced, the mathematics in $ω^ω$ terms (?) becomes complicated.

As pieces of the Ball banged out, unsaturated yins and yangs in the pieces would continue to multiply, to saturate, and to explode (sub-Bang) one generation every nearotime. However, multiplication must cease at some point. Presumably, unsaturated yins and yangs would not explode, but all saturated yins and yangs would. The late stage of the Bang would therefore be critical to the varieties of the strands, their mix, and the final mass of the Universe. It is hard to surmise whether mathematical modeling would shed light on the theoretical quantity of the *finite* Universe.

As noted, the yin-yang duos are practically empty gestalts. The spheres of the individual yins and yangs are not mutually exclusive. The more tightly yins and yangs pack, the more their spheres overlap, and the greater the pressure that would build up. How many yangs could pack around a yin (namely, the number ω) is indeterminate, considering that yins and yangs are tiny *nearo nonbeings* or *sub-beings* of practical nothingness.

GESTALT DYNAMICS

Gestaltation creates something not found in its composition or sum. The electrons and the nucleus are not the atoms; their gestalt makes the atom. It is likewise for the molecules and the celestial bodies. A sodium atom and a chlorine atom (both ions being gestalts themselves) gestaltate to make a salty molecule. Since the Bang, the strands and their gestalts incessantly re-gestaltate. Consequentially, physics is a study of constant change, with constantly changing "constants," such as the light-year and the speed of light. Although yins and yangs of the Universe *in toto* sum to zero, the strands and their gestalts, like atoms, molecules, planets, stars, and constellations, are not nil. They are real to us and to all sentients. See Section II, "The Mind Gestalt."

Gestalts keep undergoing re-gestaltation. On Earth, the re-gestaltation of air and water makes winds and hurricanes. The re-gestaltation of electrons makes lightning. The re-gestaltation of people causes revolutions. Of particular importance to humanity are the mind gestalts. Mind gestalts of *Homo sapiens* further make wisdom, civilization, and culture. See Section II.

NO STRAIGHT LINE, LEVEL PLANE, TRUE CIRCLE, SYMMETRY

A line is a transient gestalt between any two points, such as between two apples or between two galaxies. Ultimately, lines are lines of strands. Drawn on paper, a line can look quite "straight." Real lines, however, cannot be straight, because strands between any two points are mobile and subject to gravity and re-gestaltations. In daily life, we perceive the path of a bullet and a jet of water as straight if point-blank but as a trajectory if at a distance. When we go "straight" from Rome to Paris, we curve not only along the surface of Earth but also around the sun on the spiraling Earth. See "Spiraling Photons" below. No one can go to Mars "straight."

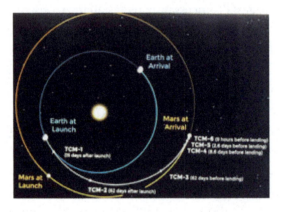

Figure: NASA photo, curvy trajectory of *Perseverance* to Mars

Because of a lack of constancy and straightness, no path can be exactly traced back. Scientists riding an electron orbiting (if it does, see below) the nucleus of an atom may perceive their path as a straight line. They may continue to believe so when they exit the atom to travel the galaxy riding on a photon. More likely, they feel they are stationary, as we feel on Earth. Although Earth spirals forward around the sun, we do not feel we are going anywhere, and we do not get dizzy from the spiraling and the spin. Apples on the tree do not appear to spiral around the sun either.

If space-time curves and light will bend, there can be no real straight line, level plane, planar circle, or true symmetry anywhere. From the very Beginning, yin 1 and yang 1 escaped mutual cancellation by avoiding symmetry. Further, they vibrate in a different way every time. Post-Bang, strands have branches of various lengths with yin endings and yang endings. They cannot be symmetrical.

Nor can their gestalts.

SPACETIME CURVES, LIGHT BEAMS, PARTICLES, PHOTONS

Imagine a line between two points in Space, A and B, five billion light-years apart. Where are they? Can you point to them? Can you envision a straight line to them or between them? Try to shoot a light beam from A to B. Can it go straight? The shortest line between any two points is supposedly a straight line. Could it be a space-time curve instead? Further, are there "straight" passages ("shortcuts") between any points in the curvy space-time? Or could anything be straight at all?

What is the direction of the travel of light? If nothing can confine light beams to any "straight" paths, light beams bend by default. During a solar eclipse, light beams from stars beyond bend when passing near the sun. The degree of bend should relate to the gravities of the sun and the photons (v.i.), their relative speed (v.i.), and the conditions of the surrounding sea of strands. Even when not passing heavy stars, light bends along local space-time curvatures.

Likewise, the ongoing expansion of the Universe likely also follows various space-time curves. Celestial bodies should curve the space-time lines around them in proportion to their gravitational pulls. See "Photons" below.

What is the speed of light? Along what line and vector (tangent) is this to be measured? Even if the test beam from point A completes its journey as originally assigned, it may never reach point B because *meanwhile*, the Universe is expanding, and the beam will bend. If B is a star, it must have moved and may have vanished. In a large scale, a test beam from A will not reach B except by rare chance. In a small scale, you cannot hit a photon with another photon from one meter away—certainly not by shooting "straight." After all, the direction of light and straightness are fuzzy concepts. The physics of light has not been validated between galaxies.

An alternative is to define distance by the number of strands between two points. Speed will then be the rate of change in the number of strands along a measuring line. For our daily life, however, whichever way light goes is called a straight line. The speed and direction of light are deemed constants. After all, light is the fastest, "straightest" and most "consistent" traveler known. Its changing direction and speed are of no daily concern or discern.

The Gestalt theory might explain why photons are light and stable and why light beams are steady and fast, *relatively*. As strands are asymmetric with yin endings and yang endings, physics of their small gestalts (*oligogestalts*, oligo-strand gestalts, gestalts of a small number of strands) will be particularly sensitive to the number of strands in the gestalt and to how the strands gestaltate among themselves. Addition, the removal or reorientation of a single strand may cause not only progressive but also quantal changes in the physics of the oligogestalts. Thus, odd-numbered and even-numbered oligogestalts may manifest as two different classes.

Further, by pairing two strands, *one this way and one the other way*, the vitality of their yin endings and yang endings will be much neutralized. The polarity, gravity, and reactivity of such a two-strand gestalt will be minimized. They would be particularly hard to tear apart. Particles consisting of or containing such stable duos will be relatively gravity-free ("light," "massless"). They would be able to travel the Sea of Strands with ease. Some may even be too light to have detectable gravity. After all, photons are "light," in English.

To generalize, such low-gravity particles may *reversibly* gestaltate themselves onto atomic electrons or other particles as "gravityless" (not *massless*) quanta. This might also be how light is emitted. Further, this may imply that *not all* physical bodies have gravity proportional to how many strands they hold. In other words, the mass-gravity relationship may vary if mass means the quantity of strands a physical body holds. Conceivably, physics of particles like protons, neutrons, and electrons might be functions of the *composition and gestaltation of the strands* they hold. Photons of various strand composition and gestaltation will vary in energy level (vibration, wavelength), but they travel at the same speed, relayed from strand to strand the same way.

Along the same line of reasoning, the pre-Bang Ball held practically equal numbers of yins and yangs and should have no gravity toward other Balls or other universes, if any. Our Universe should *likewise* have no gravity *externally measurable at a distance*. Multiple universes, if any, will have no gravitational interactions among themselves. We cannot tell the existence of other universes, if any, not only because we have no way to probe them but also because universes are mutually gravityless—namely, "dark."

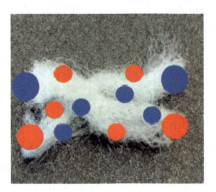

Figure. Two strands illustrating how they can gestaltate to minimize ("internalize") gravity and maximize stability. Blue dots and red dots represent yin endings and yang endings of the strands. The white-fabric cords represent the core string of the strands. The more similar the two strands, the more stable and "massless," or "dark," the duo can be.

As also hypothesized, however, strands of yins and yangs cannot be symmetrical. Therefore, no gestalts in the Universe can be totally gravity-free. The relative contributions of gravity and the space-time curvature to the bending path of light beams is hard to assess. It is also hard to speculate whether, in light beams, photons themselves move forward in the Sea of Strands or, more expeditiously, only their energy is relayed forward from strands to strands, as seen in Newton's cradles. The latter case implies that some small freestanding gestalts in the Sea of Strands might bear resemblances to photons. They might even be stock photons ("photons in reservoir"). Finally, traveling photons that do not land on matter or other gestalts might just return to the Sea of Strands and appear to "vanish." Or else, where do the photons from all the stars disappear to?

Variable Time, Clock, Light-Year, E/M Ratio

A clock is a recurrent gestalt that marks local time, as observed when subatomic particles oscillate, pendulums swing, Earth spins, and galaxies swirl. In the curvy space-time, all dimensions are local, relative, and temporary. One light-year is an approximate distance based on the assumption that the speed of light and the "year" are constant. Neither is—far from it.

As ventured above, distance can be defined by the number of strands standing between two measuring points along a measuring line. Even then, distance and time are inconstant. Every round, Earth spins and spirals around the sun a different way, resulting in a different year time. The sun itself moves too. In telling the time, we are only timing one gestaltation with another, like timing ticks with tocks. The ultimate clock of the Universe is the rhythmicity of the strands. The travel of light and intra-atomic events are good proxies. The year that we use as calendar are among the ficklest of cosmic cycles. Nothing is fickler, except the moon, the weather, and the human whims.

At the Bang, pieces of the Ball banged out into the true Void unrestricted and against no impedance except the gravitational pulls among themselves. On the way out, sub-explosions continued to push its frontline sub-pieces faster and faster. The resulting speed head was fast beyond measure, not even measurable with light. To wit, our observable Universe alone has expanded to a diameter greater than 90 billion light-years in its 13.8 billion years of existence. Post-Bang, light travels in traversed voids, mediated and restricted by strands. As a result, the speed of light becomes limited and variable with the local sea of strands. The E/M ratio, based on $E=mc^2$, where c is speed of light, likewise varies. As said above, the relationship between mass and gravity may vary too.

DATING THE UNIVERSE AND LOCATING REMOTE GALAXIES: A LONG VIEW

To estimate the age and size of the Universe, as well as the motion and evolution of remote galaxies, cosmic radiations that have meandered billions of light-years through

A Gestalt Theory of the Universe and the Mind

thick and thin will not give us straight answers. Measuring whirling galaxies from our tiny spiraling planet Earth adds uncertainty. We cannot even measure the distance between two galaxies *center to center*. Nevertheless, we have been told that our Universe is 13.8 billion years old, that it is still expanding, and that lights from some remote galaxies are 10 billion years old. These scientific data are not cast in stone nor numbered in strands.

Redshift studies examine only very short segments of light beams, as seen by us now from planet Earth. As light bends, we might be measuring it tangentially. Since the light was emitted, the remote galaxy must have moved. We have moved too. The speed and direction of motion of the galaxies could not have been constant for the ten billion years past. The spiral arms of galaxies are spiraling, not extending straight out. Imagine: light beams bend measurably, even during the short time when they pass by our tiny sun! The ultradeep cosmic lights we see today must have bent much more during the billions of years past when they meandered through massive celestial bodies. Therefore, a galaxy that appears ten billion light-years away in one direction might actually have moved to our neighborhood in another direction or vanished.

As galaxies whirl, any frequency shifts detected from inside the Universe are only as accurate as the local weather report. Whether the Universe is expanding or shrinking can be best determined from outside of the Universe, an impossible feat. The alternative is to make references to the center of the Universe, an unknown

Tainan Lee 李清木

place, or to map the density and scatter of the strands. Unfortunately, the strands are too small to study, and we cannot send test beams straight to a galaxy and bring them back to check things out.

Furthermore, if the pieces of the exploding Ball banged out at a speed faster than light, we can never see the other hemi-Universe. Our observable universe is only a crooked peephole view of a very small portion of our mobile Subverse.

Suppose we see ten-billion-year-old light from a remote galaxy today. Suppose further that the galaxy still exists, and that its light will continue to come "straight" to us in the same direction. We will then be able to see it *in its new lights* for another ten billion years, if not more. If the galaxy had vanished four billion years ago, we would still be able to see its *newer* lights for another six billion years. To make sure that it did not vanish nine billion years ago, we must witness its light for another one billion years. Good luck, *Homo sapiens!* In year 1 billion+2021, the smartest sentient on planet Earth then might be a *Rattus sapiens* or a wise octopus in an undersea metropolis.

Figure: *Rattus*, not yet sapient

We may be seeing double! As the celestial bodies whirl, one remote galaxy may shine upon us more than once. For example, we may see the same galaxy simultaneously as two different ones today by seeing its ten-billion-year-old lights in one direction and its five-billion-year-old lights in another direction. The two images will differ. One is five billion years older than the other. One may look like a decaying crab, the other like an aggressive scorpion. We can compare their claws but cannot figure out that they are *one and same.* Further, an "ultradeep universe" that we see today might be our own childhood photos in the scenario that we shot away at a speed faster than light at the Big Bang, and now our own old lights are catching up with us. There may be fewer galaxies in existence than meet the eye or the telescope!

The Swirling Universe and Subverses

It is hard to imagine that anything in our ever-changing Universe will keep its original straight-out expansion course for 13.8 billion years. As galaxies whirl, the Universe swirls. We are in a spiral arm of our galaxy, and our galaxy may be in a spiral arm of the Universe. A redshift may mean only that our spiraling arm is elongating along our spiral line of vision. Maybe the dense head of our Subverse is being sucked in faster than we are, while the trailing tail of our Subverse is being sucked in slower than we are. We cannot tell whether we are swirling in or spinning out because we cannot discern minute differences in redshifts looking ahead versus looking behind. We cannot even define our curvy viewing line.

An expanding Universe has serious consequences. Until the Bang is checked by gravity, the expansion will continue. There is nothing else in the Void to stop the expansion. In a vicious cycle, the expansion of the Universe will thin out the strands, and reduced gravity will facilitate further expansion. Eventually, the whole Universe may evaporate. Will this happen? Well, we can never tell.

But as long as the galaxies appear around the same billions of light-years from us, the *expansion in our vicinity won't vaporize us during our times.* Further, whirling means that the celestial bodies in our Subverse are no longer expanding straight out. Rather than evaporating, being sucked into a blackhole could be a deeper concern.

Figure. Swirling is common among large gestalts. NASA photos: Migrating hurricane, *LU*; spiraling celestial bodies, *RU, LL*; gravitational fields of colliding black holes, *RL*.

Domino Chain Reactions, Traveling Cosmic Lights

Domino chain reactions can be amazingly sophisticated. Each display is a one-time event, a *gestalt* event. The size and shape of the dominoes may vary; so may the pace and direction of the relay. The chain reaction can progress through awesome turns.

Figure: Segment of an educational domino display of *Hevesh 5*.

Compare the dominoes' chain reaction to the strands relaying light. "Local observers" along the path of the chain, such as a smart ant on the floor, will likely perceive the speed and direction of the dominoes' progression as constant and straightforward. We can examine the collapse of a few dominoes and apply advanced mathematics to study a remote domino of our favor. Voilà! Domino X collapsed one thousand dominoes ago, and the entire chain consists of 13.8 hundred dominoes. However, if we would just take a look around, rather than trying to backtrack the chain scientifically, we may see that Domino X actually lies just around the corner. Backtracking the cosmic lights through a peeping hole and assuming that lights travel straight at a constant speed, we likewise calculate that light from Galaxy X started ten billion years ago "straight toward us." We further determine that the Universe is 13.8 billion years old. Something wrong?

There is no chance that a remote galaxy would stay in the direction of a viewing telescope for ten billion years. Unfortunately, we cannot tell its past and present locations, relative to ours or relative to the center of the Universe. As we receive photons from a remote galaxy, we cannot tell how the light has meandered around before reaching us. We are bound to err, especially if we assume that light travels straight at a constant speed.

ATOMIC ELECTRONS, HOPPING SPIRALING PHOTONS, HOPPING TIME

Atomic electrons are thought to appear by probability at various locations on appropriate "orbits" around the nucleus. Conceivably, free strands surround the nucleus. Electrons gestaltate around the nucleus and jump from strand to strand around the nucleus at layers appropriate to their quantal energy. When electrons hop *in a layer*, the "orbit" is roughly round. When electrons cover *different layers*, the "orbit" would be elliptical.

A Gestalt Theory of the Universe and the Mind

When liberated from the atom, photons likely shoot forward as particles, hopping along *in layers* of strands as if still riding on the electrons. They spiral, thereby defining a tubal path. Nothing confines them to a planar sinusoidal path crossing the center of the path every cycle. To reconcile, it is noted that Newton's cradle is a still lineal model, whereas the stands vibrate three dimensionally and the photons hop forward in a tubal path.

Across the tube, photons hop like *particles*; along the tube, they travel like a *wave*.

Time hops too. The nearotime in the Ball and the rhythmic dance of the strands in the Universe are *discrete, indivisible time units*. The collapse of each domino and the strand-to-strand relay are discrete events, too. To these events, the past, the present, and the future are discrete epochs, epoch by epoch. Time only marks events. It ticks and tocks forward at a pace appropriate to the events it is marking, such as a year, a month, a day, a pendulum swing, an atomic shake, a wiggle of the strand, or a jerk of a yin-yang duo.

As traveling photons hop from strand to strand, what makes us see continuity is the overlapping of gestalts. Like in a movie, each picture frame is discrete, but the overlapping visual mind gestalts give us the perception of continuity. In our daily life, time feels continuous because we pool random overlapping events together. All successive events become continuous in blurred view perceived by a slow mind. The action potentials of the visual neurons are discrete all-or-nothing events. It is the pooled synaptic action potentials (that make up our visual gestalts) that give us a sense of continuity. There is more on this in "The Mind Gestalts," Section II.

In our real world, things also tend to spiral forward. Spiraling gives "elasticity" to the beam so that it will bend smoothly and easily without kinking. Earth spirals as it orbits the sun. Hurricanes and tornados whirl. Bullets travel best spiraling—so do the cochlea in the inner ear, DNA, grape tendrils, and advancing screws function better spiraling. Deviation from the spiral path costs energy.

Figure: Spirals on Earth and in heaven: a flat snail, *LU*; a pointed shell, *UR*; a NASA cosmic image, *LL*; NASA view of the spiraling path of Earth around the sun, *RL*

It is interesting that the English letters *e*, *m*, and *w* (energy, matter, work) in *cursive writing* feel like spirals, clockwise (*m*) or counterclockwise (*e, w*).

Beyond Sciences, Philosophy

THINGS MAY NOT BE WHAT they appear or mean to be. The seas of strands are liquid gravitational fields in space-time. The passage of each energy particle is unique, ephemeral, and cannot be backtracked. We can detect redshifts of lights now, but we cannot determine their relative wavelengths over the past billions of years, nor into the future. Traces of cosmic lights reach us by a very small chance after a very long, convoluted journey. Just like the chains of dominoes, short segments of lights do not tell us about their whole journey and less about the truth of the Universe. Sections of spirals and curves will appear straight if short enough. Vice versa, long stretches tend to blur out minor bends.

OUR SUBVERSE: ITS PAST, ITS PRESENT, ITS MYSTERIES

The 10-billion-year-old light we see today from a remote galaxy started its journey before our sun was born 4.6 billion years ago. It did not shine upon us; we moved *accidentally* into its path to be enlightened. The galaxy itself might have vanished. (See "Dating the Universe" above.) The light has bounced through *thick and thin* on a convoluted journey. It hits the Hubble by a small chance during a very short window of time when we happen to be on Earth.

Where are we? As stated above, we would be able to tell the present state of the Universe only by sending test beams straight to the remote galaxies and bringing back current information right away. Better yet, we could take a look from outside the Universe. Both being scientifically impossible, the rest is up to philosophy. After all, ever since *Homo sapiens* began to think, philosophy, fantasy, and religions have always gone hand in hand with sciences—if not ahead of sciences. No wonder a doctoral degree in sciences is commonly called a PhD, or Doctor of Philosophy. Philosophy probes beyond what sciences can prove. In an ever-changing universe, it is naive to believe that photons travel without medium, straight, and with invariable speed forever. Even with great sciences, our knowledge is limited. Forecasting the fate of the Universe from tentative earthly discoveries is no more reliable than predicting global warming with a drop of morning dew.

NASA offers amazing pictures taken by the Hubble Space Telescope that enable astronomers to construct bright scientific views of the solar system, the Milky Way, and the Universe. Interested laypersons can also learn that (1) lights that the Hubble detects from the near galaxies, the deep galaxies, and the ultradeep galaxies are about 0.8 to 3 billion, 3 to 7 billion, and 7 to 13 billion years old, respectively, (2) the lights from the farthest galaxies are so redshifted that they look red, and (3) the more remote from us the galaxies are, the more primitive they appear. (Source: YouTube, Deep Universe: Hubble's Universe Unfiltered)

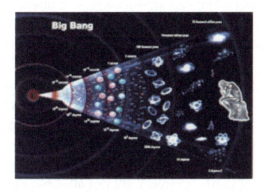

Figure: NASA photo illustrating the extreme deep, the ultradeep, the deep, and the near galaxies in the *observable* universe. Note that the x-axis shows time from the Big Bang. The conical picture is not meant to depict a cone of the present-day universe. We only have a peep-hole view.

Take the case of the ultradeep galaxies whose 10-billion-year-old light we see today (when the Universe is 13.8 billion years old, and our Milky Way Galaxy is 13.6 billion years old). Allowing for inaccuracies, these galaxies and our Milky Way are close *contemporaries*. Over the past ten billion years, our galaxy has evolved. We now have Earth and us. The ultradeep galaxies we left behind must have evolved as well. Who knows what they have today? Do they still shine? Do their stars and planets harbor civilization? To find out for sure, we must wait for ten billion years for their new lights of today to reach us. Our sun will not last that long. *Homo sapiens* cannot do it. Can any omniscient help us?

While making great discoveries, cosmological sciences also create amazing mysteries. Cosmic light from every galaxy we see is red-shifting. Every way the Hubble Space Telescope looks, it is looking into the past (for "*the future is not ours to see*"). If you turn the Hubble the other way, you will still see old galaxies with similar stories. Therefore, everything is moving away from everything else as the universe expands in every direction. All considered, if the universe is "homogenous and isotropic," it does not have a center. Well, not all these deductions make common sense, do they? We used to believe that Earth is flat, without a center.

Now the universe has no center?! Didn't the Big Bang explode *inside out* from a center? If celestial bodies are "spiraling" all around us, no path can be straight, and "this way" curves into "the other way." When we cannot discern minor differences in redshifts this way versus the other way, we lose a fine sense of direction. A common person like me can more easily grasp a roughly round Universe, with a center, with all galaxies suspended in the Sea of Strands, in which our observable Subverse spirals and expands all around us in our vicinity. Or are we in the center of the Universe?

EMPTINESS, INCONSTANCY, CONSERVATION OF STRANDS

Except for one nearotime when yin 1 was alone, the pre-Universe and the Universe have been balanced gestalts of zero-sum. Considering how small the Ball was and how violently it exploded, the observable Universe is practically empty. So are the strands, the particles, the atoms, and the galaxies.

It is enlightening that Buddha realized the nothingness of the Universe some twenty-six hundred years ago. The Heart Sutra clearly says, "Formed beings differ not from emptiness, emptiness differs not from formed beings. Feelings, thoughts, deeds, senses, likewise" (心經:「色不異空，空不異色」。「受想行識, 亦復如是」). However, all "empty" things appear and feel so real to us, the earthly mortals. *Reconciling nothingness and realness, everything is real as a gestalt.* A yin-yang duo is a gestalt; the Universe is a gestalt. So is everything in between. Gestalts are real, especially when realized by mind gestalts. See "The Mind Gestalts," Section II.

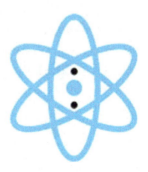

Figure: Yin and yang, black dots, gestaltate to become a being. The duo occupies a space that is practically empty.

Buddha also emphasized that everything is ever-changing and inconstant. In concordance, strands and gestalts keep undergoing re-gestaltation. For practical purposes, we take the speed and direction of travel of light as constants and use them to calibrate dimensions. However, if our sun, small as it is, is big enough to bend the passing beams of light, stars billions of times larger can bend passing light beams much more acutely. As said above, true constants were lost with the Bang. As a photon travels from a star to Earth, it makes the star a little smaller and Earth a little larger by a quantum of sorts. There can be no constancy in the Universe except constant change.

The law of conservation of energy-matter states that energy-matter does not vanish or get created. However, if strands may gestaltate to become energy-matter, and vice versa, the law of conservation may mean that the total amount of strands in the Universe will not change. Following "Formed beings differ not from emptiness, emptiness differs not from formed beings," the Heart Sutra says, "Nothing born, nothing vanishes." This could mean a law of conservation at the level of the strands. See "The Fate of the Universe" above for the case of yin-yang annihilation.

HUMANITY, MIND, FENG SHUI, YIN-YANG CULTURE

The Earth has unique gestalts of weather, biology, humanity, and civilization. On Earth, biological materials gestaltate to make life. Sentients communicate by moving gestalts of air molecules to make sounds to the ears. In the brain, the neurons organize into anatomical gestalts to generate physiological gestalts of synaptic action potentials, which make up the mind gestalts. Among mind gestalts are senses, sensation, knowledge, spirit, awareness, thoughts, and wisdom. See "The Mind Gestalts," Section II. Mind gestalts transcend physics. Thoughts like "Cogito, ergo sum," opined by the great philosopher Descartes, seem to authenticate mind gestalts as the basis for *sum* ("I am").

Asian culture appreciates feng shui (風水), which is the gestalt energy derived from how things are arranged and how qi (氣) permeates through furniture, buildings, people, mountains, and valleys.

Good feng shui gestalts generate positive energy.

In life, yin-yang gestalts are ubiquitous. A man-woman gestalt has something beyond the man and the woman. In gestalt, mountains, rivers, trees, animals, paintings, and groups of people generate something not found in the components, individually or in sum.

Lao Tzu (老祖, Lao Zi, 老子), the founder of Taoism, preached yin-yang harmony and emphasized the harmonious gestaltation of man and the environment. What foresight! A harmonious, stress-free mental state enhances personal health and societal orderliness. In still rendering, yin-yang harmony is customarily depicted as yin and yang sharing a planar circle. It could be better presented in 3-D and dynamically. See also "The Creation: The Yin-Yang 凹凸 Gestalt" above.

 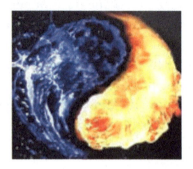

Figure: Yin-yang harmony in 2-D and quasi-3D renderings

THE EXTRATERRESTRIALS AND OUR SPACE NEIGHBORHOOD

When we talk about extraterrestrials (ETs), we talk about super intelligent sentients that are smart enough to find us. *Unlikely!*

Consider that we have not found them and consider further what a miracle it has been for *Homo sapiens* to be here today. Civilization is only thousands of years old. High technology capable of probing the Space is only decades old. It is by a very rare combination of extreme lucks that we become what we are today. It has taken Earth over four billion years to have smart *Homo sapiens* for just twenty thousand years. Only sixty-five million years ago, life on Earth was decimated, along with the extinction of dinosaurs. The astronauts first landed on the moon only fifty years ago.

Compare timelines side by side. *ET sapiens* and *Homo sapiens* flourishing together in the same neighborhood during our time is too rare a coincidence to occur. If their technology is one hundred years behind us, they cannot signal to us their presence. If their technology is one hundred years ahead of us, they may want to raid us to replenish their resources. For a brief update on the search for extraterrestrial life, see *the Wall Street Journal*, March 30, 2021, R. L. Hotz's: "The Search for Alien Life Ramps Up." If life does exist beyond Earth, scientists say they may find a trace of it soon. However, so-called "signs of life" could be billions of years away from intelligence and civilization, considering that life started on Earth 3.6 billion years ago.

Special radars and telescopes around the world are searching for telegram-like signals from ETs. However, across the seas of strands of light-year dimensions, a few photons from them will unlikely tick our receivers.

Might the ETs "discover" us? The oceans, the land, the air, the plants, and the animals we have on Earth are extremely precious properties, not easily found, even in the heavens. Hopefully, no ETs will need these earthly treasures of ours. Pray that they cannot find our Earth and do not need our flesh and blood for nutritional supplements to enhance their immunity against their coronaviruses.

Tainan Lee 李清木

Figure: NASA photo, the Milky Way. Our Sun is too small to see. Can the ETs find us?

Should we meet ETs, what might happen? We tend to depict them to be like us. We cannot be more wrong! They may have two big eyes for lights. They may not need two legs or two hands of five fingers each. They may have no ears and no voices like ours, for they may not have an atmosphere like ours. Our life is carbon based; theirs may be sulfur based. That stinks! Do they sniff with noses? Their body temperature may be two hundred degrees hotter than ours—too hot to kiss. They may use a different light spectrum and may be fluorescent. They may weigh five thousand pounds, or five pounds, with an absurd specific gravity. Their IQ may be 5,000, for if they have IQ like ours or less, they will have no ability to come to find us first. Furthermore, we may not understand their number systems.

With ten fingers, we figure with a decimal number system. Who knows how the ETs do their mathematics! Their minds may outdo our supercomputers. With advanced brain-computer interface (BCI), they may not even need fingers to control their computers. Ultimately, ETs could be just fat lumps of neurons in gestalt. With advanced mind gestalts (Section II), they may need very few body parts. As mortals, though, they do need something for subsistence and for pleasure. After all, what is a mortal life all about?

Figure: An ET, depicted like a skinny, ugly man, perhaps hungry and greedy too. Look into those eyes! Do you trust him or her?

SAVE OUR PLANET EARTH

Habitable planets are supposed to exist around suns within twenty light-years of our sun. However, exoplanets with "favorable" conditions for life are at least one hundred light-years away. Even then, can we travel that light-year distance *alive*? Being habitable does not mean it is good enough for you to want to move there. At home, we have the most valuable real estate—*rare* estate, indeed! Before you buy your ticket to emigrate, remember that it took *Perseverance* six months to travel two hundred million kilometers to Mars, and a light-year is nine trillion kilometers. It is very cold in the Outer Space, at -270 degrees C, and it is dark between suns. You may see no sun light for thousands of generations. Your offspring will be deaf and blind. Finally, if you give up, turn around, and make it back to Earth alive, you will have to learn a new language to live in a new civilization, if any exists. You will be ET to *Homo neo sapiens*! Beware, you will lose neurons during your long hangout in Space (ref., J. Daley, *Smithsonian Magazine*, October 2018). Not very smart.

We *Homos sapiens* should be better off taking good care of our home, Earth, rather than attempting to emigrate to another planet or to rob from any *Extraterrestrial sapiens*. Unfortunately, humans may be too destructive to evade self-destruction. Albert Einstein has been quoted as saying that he knew not how World War III would be fought, but he knew that Would War IV would be fought with stones and sticks—no more high tech. For reference, the Stone Age ended five thousand years ago with the invention of bronze. Dinosaurs vanished seventy-five million years ago. Multicellular life forms emerged on Earth about one billion years ago. Decades of high tech have not established man's durability on Earth, less on some remote, desolate, frigid, loveless, strange planet called Mars.

A planet underfoot is better than two in the heavens. Nowhere else can we build a colony with good amenities, even if we export a major portion of the Earth's air, water, and organic resources to a habitable exoplanet. Not worth it! If you are eager to live in paradise, make Earth one, pray for "thy kingdom come," or bet on a good afterlife. See Section II.

Figure: NASA photo, planet Earth, the rarest prime real estate

Tainan Lee 李清木

Figure. A planet underfoot is better than two in the heavens. Treasures found only on Earth: Loving ducks, *LU*; the Grand Canyon, *RU*; dragon fruit flower, *LL*; rolling hill by Pacific Ocean, *RL*

Section II: The Mind Gestalts

A Gestalt Theory of Their Formation and Function
結搭心靈說

Abstract 59
Structure and Function of Mind Gestalts 61
The Neuronal and Electrophysiological Gestalts
The Mind Gestalts
The Formation and Execution of Mind Gestalts
The Multitasking Neurons
The Evolution of Mind Gestalts
The Individuality of Mind Gestalts
Sentio, Ergo Sum! The "I" Mind Gestalt
Neurology, Psychology, and Psychiatry
Physiology and Health of Mind Gestalts 73
Basal Brain Functions
Neuronal Learning and Mind Gestaltation
Age and Mind Gestaltation
Durability of Mind Gestalts
Sleeping and Dreaming as Maintenance Services

Computation of Mind Gestalts **81**
Electroencephalography and
   Magnetoencephalography (EEG and MEG)
Computer-Brain Interface (CBI)
Computed, Telemetered Mind Gestalts
Interventional Mind Gestaltation
Personal Secrets and Privacy
Uses and Abuses of Artificial Mind Gestaltation (AMG)
Anesthesia, Sedation, Therapeutic Mind Gestaltation.
Spinal Cord Electrophysiological Gestalt Therapy

Anecdotes **93**
Telepathy and Telemind
Culture, Lingering Melodies, Haunting Smiles
Wearable Mind-Controlling Headpieces

The Super-mind Gestalts **97**
The Sentience and the "I" Gestalts
The Soul Gestalt
The Sentient ID, the Karma, the Afterlife Gestalt
Deities and Our Mind Gestalts
Gestalts in the Space-Time Web

Abstract

TOGETHER, PARTS GESTALTATE (結搭) to make a dynamic whole. The gestalt holds something above and beyond the parts and their sum. Gestalt energy is ubiquitous but may not be measurable in physical terms. As I proposed in Section I, the electrons and the nucleus are not the atom; their gestalt (結搭) is the atom. In the Universe, the strands gestaltate and re-gestaltate to become subparticles, photons, energy-matter, stars, and galaxies. Everything in the Universe, including the Universe itself, is a gestalt. So is the mind.

All living sentients sense and interact with their environment. The central nervous system and the minds of humans are among the most complex and advanced of all gestalts on planet Earth. The neurons are strategically arranged in ganglia, gyri, nuclei, lobes, and hemispheres for efficient generation of complex gestalts of synaptic action potentials that consist of the brain waves and the mind gestalts. The neuronal gestalts overlap, commingle, and intertwine extensively but maintain operational orders; so do the mind gestalts. The mind gestalts are ephemeral but can be remembered as recallable synaptic gestalts. Day and night, the synaptic gestalts are active, working, or undergoing repair and maintenance. Mind gestalts not only interact with the environment but also enable self-awareness, wisdom, and intelligence. They are vehicles for sentience, spirit, philosophy, knowledge, humanity, and soul.

Future research may enable advanced computer-brain interfaces, mind gestalt analyses and manipulations, and therapeutic mind re-gestaltations.

To the sentients, what the mind gestalts recognize is what is real, including the unique sense of "self." *Sentio, ergo sum!* Especially intriguing are the super-mind gestalts, including the deities, the sentience gestalt, the "I" gestalt, and the karma gestalt.

Structure and Function of Mind Gestalts

The Neuronal and Electrophysiological Gestalts
IN OUR BRAINS, BILLIONS OF neurons are strategically stacked in smart anatomical gestalts, like ganglia, nuclei, gyri, lobes, and hemispheres.

Figure: Gross anatomy, surface gyri of the human brain

Structure facilitates function. A neuron has tens of hundreds of dendrites equipped with functional units and synapses. Simplistically put, a synapse is a sophisticated gating structure. Neurons compute incoming signals and generate outgoing action potentials. An action potential itself is a complex influx and efflux of ions across the cell membrane in a dynamic time course. Unlike a motor neuron that controls a discrete motor unit of contractile muscle cells through one axon, a cerebral neuron functions by complex multitasking and networking. In the brain, synapses constantly gestaltate and re-gestaltate to produce gestalts of synaptic action potentials that constitute the mind.

THE MIND GESTALTS

A basic mind gestalt may be illustrated by the recognition of a line or a triangle. Whereas a solo point in the Void is undefinable, two points gestaltate to define a line, and three points gestaltate to define a triangle and a plane. Further, seeing three dots excites a group of retinal neurons to form a corresponding gestalt of retinal action potentials, which travels up the visual cortex. Receiving neurons in the cortex formulate new gestalts to recognize the triangle and analyze its size, shape, and color. Under various circumstances, a gestalt of three dots may elicit a variety of secondary neuronal, synaptic, cognizant, intellectual, and even emotional gestalts. A triangle may be remembered and stored as a recallable synaptic gestalt. Our mind gestalts can be visual, auditory, emotional, or intellectual. As human creativity, they can also be assembled *de novo* by internal working without external input.

Figure. A live mind gestalt can be likened to a bonfire.

A live mind gestalt can be likened to a flame, a bonfire, a puff of smoke, or a cloud. In a flame, numerous combustible molecules combine with oxygen. In a mind gestalt, numerous neuronal synapses generate action potentials in dynamic, complex, but orderly gestaltations. In both cases, the gestalts are 4-D space-time compositions of numerous individual events. Gestaltation makes continuity out of discrete events. Patterns, flows, and shapes of gestaltation take on extra meanings above and beyond their components and sum. In the brain, vision, cognition, emotion, judgment, volition, a command to fight or flight, memory, and so forth are all mind gestalts that can occur simultaneously and sequentially. Mind gestalts readily overlap, interact and re-gestaltate among themselves. For illustration, pitching a baseball involves the thinking, seeing, aiming, throwing, and balancing of many mental and physical gestalts. Playing a concerto on stage requires a sustained movielike rendering and execution of a massive number of mind gestalts after mind gestalts.

The Formation and Execution of Mind Gestalts
Unique to the brain are its abilities to remember and to reason. Knowledge and memory are stored mind gestalts that can be rekindled. Reasoning and creativity are generations of new mind gestalts based on stored mind gestalts, with or without additional inputs.

Various mind gestalts take on different characteristics. For example, audio mind gestalts can be recalled and sung; visual mind gestalts can be re-envisioned. Mind gestalts can even be construed creatively. To train is to teach the mind how to compose and execute better mind gestalts for a prettier painting, a better song, a higher jump, or a better business plan. An improved martial art posture facilitates the delivery of a faster and sharper punch under the control of refined mind gestalts. A good joke can trigger a pleasant mind gestalt that effectuates a hearty laugh.

Han Chinese people describe nostalgic memories of the past as "like thin smoke (如煙)," with a feeling of nostalgia and loss.

Mind gestalts work both internally and externally.

Even during sleep, mind gestalts patrol the mind and the body and monitor for inputs. A person in depression churns miserable thoughts over and over again. A philosopher squeezes existing mind gestalts to create new ideas. The survival instinct of "fight or flight" entails the quick execution of numerous mind gestalts that control visualization, interpretation, judgment, emotion, body motion, and sympathetic nervous functions. Volitional activities are executed by will-directed motor mind gestalts.

Mind gestalts tend to repeat, extend, and facilitate themselves. That is how "practice makes perfect," and knowledge builds upon knowledge. When mind gestalts repeat themselves, good habits make life and learning effortless; bad habits tend to become difficult to correct.

THE MULTITASKING NEURONS

Each neuron has many dendrites and synapses. This means many gestalts share many neurons, with overlapping routes. How many synapses a neuron can fire at a time and how fast a neuron can refire are amazing biological properties.

As mind gestalts share multitasking neurons, gestalts ignite gestalts all over the brain with intertwining routing. Considering that each neuron has hundreds or thousands of synapses, many routes and segments will be heavily trafficked and shared. Efficient multitasking enables a conductor to simultaneously read and turn the music sheets, listen to many instruments, conduct with both hands and more, sense player and audience responses, execute sensational musical dynamics, and still think ahead of the music.

The extensive neuronal inter-routing and code sharing not only enable the "normal" vivid wakefulness but also cause illogical experiences during dreams (see "Sleeping and Dreaming as Maintenance Services"). It further predisposes the mind to psychological and mental illnesses.

The Evolution of Mind Gestalts

The numbers of neurons and synapses of many animals have been studied and published on the internet. Along the evolutionary tree, an animal brain may have just a ganglion with a few neurons or up to one hundred billion neurons in *Homo sapiens* (twenty-five billion in the cerebral cortex). Trillions of synapses exist in our central nervous system. As a result, the multiplicity and complexity of mind gestalts are unfathomable. For as long as a brain lives, its neurons are busy receiving inputs and making and relaying mind gestalts.

For information, an ant has 250,000 brain neurons, a mouse 70 million, a rat 200 million, a cat 750 million, and an adult human close to 200 billion. Among mammals, African elephants have more total neurons than humans, while long-finned pilot whales have more neurons in the cerebral cortex (source: Wikipedia, *List of animals by number of neurons*).

A Gestalt Theory of the Universe and the Mind

With evolution, not only do more neurons become available, but the improved architecture of the brain also facilitates faster and more efficient routing and multitasking. Some animals are particularly smart, relative to the size of their brains. Crows are well illustrated in fables for their creativity. Octopuses are heroes of modern intelligence research. Their neurons and synapses must have uniquely superior anatomical and functional qualities, or these structures must be arranged in unusually efficient gestaltations.

Octopuses supposedly dispatch a major portion of their neurons to the arms so that each arm acts with some intelligence of its own. Among people, these structural and functional variations likely also differentiate geniuses versus the ordinary, the learned versus the illiterate, and the healthy versus the mentally ill.

All sentient animals sense, interpret, and react to their environments. Even earthworms have significant neuronal and synaptic electrophysiological gestalts. In humans, the brain also stores experience and knowledge and functions as vehicles of spirit, wisdom, emotion, and creativity. Animals grouped together will learn from similar experiences and develop similar mind gestalts among themselves. Human groups have group-specific language, camaraderie, culture, values, goals, etiquette, and belief.

In specific gestalts, neurons are specialized to perform specific tasks such as hearing, smelling, remembering or thinking. As a result of specialization, geniuses can excel in specific things like art, music, or abstract thinking, but some of them may have a hard time learning mundane daily tasks. I know of a math genius who still needs his mother to tie his shoelaces on his way to Harvard.

The Individuality of Mind Gestalts

Even as everyone looks at the same moon, *everyone sees a different moon every time.* By the time the moonlight reaches the retina, the clouds, the cornea, the lenses, and the vitreous have changed how the light hits the retinal neurons. Then, considering how the neurons, dendrites, and synapses gestaltate differently among people and how action potentials consist of moving ions, the mind gestalt anyone generates of a moon can never be the same as that of anyone else. We tell one another that we see the same moon, but we generate different mind gestalts every time. We even have dissimilar emotional reactions.

Moonlight is particularly able to generate homesickness and lovesickness for wanderers. The formation and appreciation of such mind gestalts vary with culture and times.

At the level of the mind gestalt, everything is ephemeral, and every gestalt is different. Likewise, a cock's crow may elicit different mind gestalts in different brains. That is part of how every person has an individual personality, preferences, and peculiarities. No less than the fingerprints, the facial features, and the DNA, the mind gestalts differ from person to person. Mind gestaltation in reaction to a simple standard test may identify individuals *by their minds.*

Figure: Rainbow, moonlight, sunset, and waterfall

SENTIO, ERGO SUM! THE "I" MIND GESTALT

The sense of "I" resides deep in the mind of most sentients. The "I" gestalt is fundamental and more deeply seated than the mind gestalts of knowledge, wisdom, emotions, and intelligence. It is closely related to sentience and the soul. See also "The Super-mind Gestalts" below.

One of the greatest struggles of humanity is for man to find and recognize himself. *Am I real? Do I exist?* The great philosopher Descartes finally realized "Cogito, ergo sum" ("I think, therefore I am"). Well, my fellow commoners, wonder no more. Although the Universe sums to zero and everything seems empty, gestaltation makes things real, and mind gestalts make "I" real.

Figure. *Sentio, ergo sum*. Descartes, *LU*; a version of *The Thinker*, *RU*; a thinking gorilla, *LL*; a thinking owl blinking one eye, *RL*. For information, Auguste Rodin created the sculptural masterpiece commonly called *The Thinker*. The baby owl fell onto my tennis court. Fortunately, he figured out fast and managed to fly away safely after posting for a few courtesy pictures. He blinked one eye at a time for this photograph.

To all sentients, *Sentio, ergo sum*. Being sentient, I am real! Look closely and notice that only the sculptured *Thinker* still doubts his own realness. He has no mind gestalts. Lacking his "I" gestalt, he will never sense his own "*sum.*" All others assert "*ergo sum*" in self-realization. Without a doubt, *I am real!*

NEUROLOGY, PSYCHOLOGY, AND PSYCHIATRY
In the context of this article, neurology concerns neuronal gestaltations and their physical transcriptions. Psychology studies mind gestaltation and behavior modification. Psychiatry studies and treats pathological mind gestaltations. Mental disorders are manifestations of pathological mind gestalts due to structural or functional mis-gestaltation of the neurons and/or their synapses.

Physiology and Health of Mind Gestalts

BASAL BRAIN FUNCTIONS
Many basal functions of the central and peripheral nervous systems are hard-wired short-circuitry reflexes. These can be executed quickly without prior thinking. They include the autonomic nervous systems, the reflexes, as well as the vital activities such as breathing and swallowing. They reach out to consult with the conscious mind only when needed, post hoc.

NEURONAL LEARNING AND MIND GESTALTATION
Just like amoebas keep moving and cardiac muscle cells keep contracting, neurons keep making synapses and firing synaptic action potentials. They are social, and they like to gestaltate.

Mammalian fetal neurons are already well connected. Human newborns breathe and cry upon birth, driven by neuronal gestalts already developed, connected, and primed in utero. They hear, see, feel, and appreciate too. They have been learning all along in utero. Neurons keep learning new gestalts for as long as they are able to. Everything learned is a mind gestalt saved in the form of re-ignitable neuronal and synaptic gestalts.

AGE AND MIND GESTALTATION

In a young, growing, relatively small brain, new neurons and new synapses grow expeditiously and exponentially, neurons learn quickly, and dendrites find their way easily. Soon after birth, calves learn to stand, and all mammalian babies learn how good mother's milk is. No one doubts that they enjoy it too. Taking advantage of the well-developed and still-developing neuronal gestalts, learning continues naturally and effortlessly after birth.

As the brain grows larger, the neuronal gestalts become more complex. To make synapses, the dendrites must reach farther, go around, or negotiate through existing tangles of dendritic threads. Gestalts share neurons. As new mind gestalts become larger but less efficient and less secure, learning becomes slower. Then, after teenage, we *practically* stop making new neurons. See " Durability of Mind Gestalts" below. We even lose neurons. "Synaptic pruning" is the process by which the brain gets rid of unused synapses. As the brain further matures, learning becomes limited to finding available synapses, as well as re-gestaltation among existing gestalts of synapses.

With age, intuitions and instincts gradually give way to experience and wisdom. Learning by association means building new gestalts by extending existing gestalts. Meditation and hypnosis can facilitate the recall of dormant gestalts. In any case, learning becomes increasingly dependent on "learning how to learn" and requires more rehearsal, repetition, and reinforcement.

With further aging, fewer and fewer neurons and synapses are available. Here comes a head-on "competition of purposes." On the one hand, we try to learn new things by taking neurons and synapses from old gestalts, at the risk of sacrificing them. On the other hand, we strive to remember old essentials by making their synapses less likely to be taken away to recycle. We constantly remodel and reroute synapses, arbitraging between competing purposes. Eventually, the poor, aging mind becomes feeble, insecure, and slow.

Recent things are particularly hard for seniors to remember because the brain has to search deep, reach far through debris, and make long, convoluted detours and trade-offs to establish new connections. In senility, even well-remembered, familiar lifelong things may become hard to recall. Unfortunately, pain and suffering persist, often to hurt beyond their intended usefulness. *Oh, my!* A major source of frustration of the senior is the inability to flight or fight in the presence of a strong need and urge to do so. They often need help to fight or to flight from insecurity, incapacity, poverty, and pain. It is often remarked that old people are like kids. *With a difference!* They can barely hold on to what they learned as kids.

Sunset could be equally beautiful, but sunrise has a brighter future.

DURABILITY OF MIND GESTALTS
Neuronal and mind gestalts do deteriorate, but not in random order. Autonomic functions and quick reflexes were developed *in utero* when the connections were short, straightforward, secure, and easy to make. They usually last for life, subject to dysfunctions.

Eating, hearing, and seeing are mostly learned soon after birth, with increasingly convoluted wiring. These vital gestalts are also subject to age-related deterioration, although usually not so badly. Mind gestalts built during childhood, such as a lullaby, the national anthem, the home address, as well as parental and sibling loves, are generally remembered well into old age, even in a sickbed.

Home, sweet home!

Gestalts learned late in life are increasingly susceptible to spoilage, breakage, and pilferage. Finally, when healthy neurons and synapses become scarce, we may steadily lose our minds. New gestalts can hardly be assembled. Existing gestalts decay. Eventually, even vital functions can fail. Loss of reason, memory, judgment, and mobility may render a senior nursing home bound.

In rough times of want, healthy mind gestalts outlast life span, but in prosperous times of abundance, mind gestalts may fail to keep up with prolonged life span. The secret to a better *later life*, then, is to keep learning. Synapses that are activated remain healthier.

Regrettably, this may require setting priority to favor what we choose to keep. Prioritization and adaptation help us lead a fair late life the way we like it. Still, personality may deteriorate. Forgive the grumpy old men. If they lose more neurons and stop complaining, they soon "fall off the cliff."

Given good general health, recent research has found that the brain has certain plasticity and remains somewhat moldable, even late in life. Some new neurons are still being born. Unfortunately, healthy neuronal gestalts do not keep up forever. Sleep is particularly important for seniors to repair neuronal and mind gestalts.

Sleeping and Dreaming as Maintenance Services

The need for constant repair, cleaning, and rewiring of synaptic meshwork is obvious. It is incomprehensible that so many neurons can be strategically packed into the human brain in any logical manner. More amazingly, their synapses are connected as if terabytes of computing elements were stacked dynamically and three-dimensionally rather than in planar silicon wafers of fixed dimensions.

Tainan Lee 李清木

Everything we do and think has a corresponding mind gestalt. Everything we learned we keep as a recallable mind gestalt.

To function properly, the brain needs continual maintenance and repair. Like the defragmentation and relocation of computer bytes, but with far greater complexity, the mind gestalts take downtime to regroup, rearrange, and rewire. Mind gestalts are made and remade while neurons and synapses are born, recruited, reassigned, and replaced. Circuits must be coordinated, dead neurons and synapses replaced, inefficient circuits rewired, missing links reestablished, ineffective crossings bypassed, and confusing overlaps pruned out. Not only individual neurons and synapses, but also entire gestalts of neurons and synapses, may be revamped. Sleep is the downtime required for repair and maintenance for the neuronal and mind gestalts. Sleep disorders are major health problems. Without efficient maintenance and repair, mind gestalts worsen quickly.

During sleep, some mind gestalts may be read as dreams when they are called up for service. Recalled gestalts may be subjected to temporary detours and segregations. With disconnections and misconnections, dreams will be fragmented and irrational. Unrelated themes may be misconnected through a common link. Volition to move may be poorly channeled to motor neurons. Motions may be abrupt, jerky, awkward, and fragmented. Being unable to move in dreams can be distressful, but the ability to execute unintended movements could have worse consequences. Color and shape may not agree with reality. Long, sidelined memory may resurface.

Figure: Dreams are rarely rendered/ remembered with high fidelity.

Since dream gestaltations are not intended for learning, dreams are not well remembered. Even dreams recallable upon waking are usually forgotten soon. Dreams are rarely intellectually productive, although dreamers sometimes get a hint to their puzzles.

The all-important rapid eye movement (REM) sleep suggests that a major dream workshop is located near the neuronal cluster that moves the eyes. This could be strategically located near the midline of the brain so that dream gestalts can be brought in and out of the workshop from left and right. The side-to-side eye movement could be coincidental with the transport of dream gestalts left and right. Good REM sleep, therefore, indicates healthy maintenance services to the mind. Sleep REM is not tied to vision because even the blind can have REM sleep.

Why certain dreams keep coming back is perplexing. Strongly unpleasant experiences are particularly hard to forget. Maybe deeply emotional ("important") mind gestalts are stored near the dream workshop or the transport hub. It is commonly said that life is like a dream. It is also often felt that life is full of hardship. Therefore, if you have a good dream, appreciate it like real. A sweet kiss is a blessing, be it in a dream, in a daydream, or on real lips! A dream version of a forbidden fruit may even be less punishable.

Not only do humans dream, but other mammals dream too. Mind gestalts frequented by dreams do vary with age. The old fisherman in Hemingway's masterpiece *The Old Man and the Sea* described vividly his age-related changes in what he dreamed of.

Computation of Mind Gestalts

ELECTROENCEPHALOGRAPHY AND MAGNETOENCEPHALOGRAPHY (EEG AND MEG)

While powering brain functions, parts of the electromagnetic energy of the neurons, collectively as gestalts of synaptic action potentials, are detectable outside the brain as brain waves. Electroencephalography (EEG) samples the brain waves, just like the electrocardiography and electromyography sample the electrophysiological energies of the cardiac and the skeletal muscles. Gestaltation of the neurons far exceeds that of the cardiac and skeletal muscles in complexity and vividness. The mind gestalts are hard to study. The large size and cubic depth of the mushy brain, the regional specialization, the deep locations of brain centers, and the overlapping cortical topography make it hard to sample area-specific electroencephalograms. Although contact EEG technology has made great progress, off-skin brain wave technology remains far off. EEG signals are weak and much weaker off-skin.

EEG-sensing electrodes can be placed in brain tissue, on the surface of the brain, or on the skull (skin). With various contact electrodes, EEG records the brain waves in 2-D spikes along a timeline. It is most used in neurology, especially in the management of epilepsy. Stereo EEG (SEEG) guides the electrode implantation for surgical treatment of epilepsy. Bispectral index (BIS) is a derived index of sedation, commonly used in monitoring depth of sedation and anesthesia. Motor- and sensory-evoked action potentials are monitored during critical neurosurgeries to reduce the chances of accidental damage to neural tracts or neuronal groups around surgical sites.

Brain physiology and pathology are also studied with magnetic resonance imaging (MRI), functional magnetic resonance imaging (fMRI), and magnetoencephalography (MEG). Advanced MEG is applying SQUID (superconductive quantum interference device) technology to detect magnetic waves of the brain corresponding to the electric waves. This may someday enable off-skin brain wave reading via a helmet.

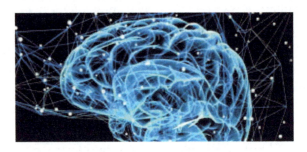

Figure. A rendition of off-surface electromagnetic energy of the brain waves (Ref. M eclipse, *Smithsonian Magazine,* January 31, 2019)

Computer-Brain Interface (CBI)

Scientific research has made great advances in CBI and has enabled some degree of mind reading. Such mind reading has enabled EEG-based telephone dialing, and mind-controlled motion of artificial limbs. It holds the promise of willful mobility for amputees and paraplegics. One is reminded that EEG is to the brain waves what music notes are to music. The 2-D music notes are not very musical, compared with the real-life symphony or the mind gestalts that it can excite. Few people enjoy reading the sheet music.

Figure. Not enjoying just reading music notes? Sing it!

Computed, Telemetered Mind Gestalts

Mind gestalts are gestalts of electromagnetic energy of the neuronal synaptic action potentials. One day,

Tainan Lee 李清木

technology may enable 3-D off-skin reading of the brain waves around the head in their real-life space-time, perhaps by using a complex high-tech helmet loaded with electric or magnetic sensors. The computerized mind gestalts might then be modulated and transmitted. Stored in silico, the recordings will outlast the aging brain.

Vice versa, computerized mind gestalts might *one day* be received directly and understood by the brain without first being translated into words, sounds, images, graphs, or movies. This can enable the blind to see and the deaf to hear, as long as their neuronal gestalts remain capable of receiving and decoding the mind gestalts. Furthermore, motor gestalts delivered to the cortex may enable a mute person to move his speech musculatures to generate speech. The helmet might work like a complex 3-D assembly of TV antennae. In computing mind gestalts, a synaptic action potential could be likened to a computer bit or byte. The possibilities of synergistic interactions between the human brain and artificial intelligence (AI) are limitless. The telepathy helmet may start with on-skin electrodes and progress to off-skin design. Its assembly of electronic gadgets can mirror actual anatomical neuronal gestaltation.

The great theoretical physicist Stephen Hawking was struck with a medical condition (ALS) that left him paralyzed. For years, his volitional movement was limited to the ability to blink eyes and move a cheek. Yet for decades, he remained a great physicist and prolific author, with the help of a word processor and speech synthesizer that read his cheek like a computer mouse. If the mind gestalts of his speech could be read and transmitted by computers, Hawking could have taught us much more about the Universe. This author and his son, among thirty-some others, have had the rare privilege and honor of experiencing weightlessness on the same "Zero-G" flight with Hawking in 2007. Supposedly, the great physicist took the weightless flight in preparation for a space journey.

EEG-based telephone dialing and artificial limb motion are *relatively* simple commands controlling simple machines to perform simple tasks. Further progress in artificial intelligence may one day permit *live* "at-will" control (without a joystick or keyboard) of robots and drones. Besides special frontlines such as deep ocean research, space exploration, space defense, and anti-terror operations, these machines could work for us *at (our) will.* Advanced AI might even decode thoughts and play them for us. Advanced electronic "mind singers" might sing aloud for us what we sing in our minds. They might also help the composers hear what they compose long before an orchestra *debuts* their opuses on stage. When I imagine a beautiful song, I would very much love to hear it right then. Wouldn't you?

The great composer Ludwig van Beethoven lost his hearing at the height of his composing career. What a tragedy! He would certainly appreciate music delivered directly to his acoustic neurons, bypassing the air, the ears, and the skull. Such pure "mind music" must be *celestial.* In a literal sense, celestial music can be heard where air does not exist, such as in heavens.

Telemetered mind gestalts (TMG) might one day connect live mind to live mind. A milestone of progress would be for a helmeted person watching a 3-D movie to transmit what he sees and hears to another helmeted person with closed eyes and plugged ears. At this level of sophistication, communication goes *mind to mind,* by helmet to helmet. True to the meaning of telepathy, separated loved ones can feel intimacy, almost as real as physical reunion.

Lovesickness can be told *mind to mind.* Such TMG also comes in handy when one is rendered speechless by strong emotions. How many times have you heard people say, "I wish I could say it better; You know what I mean?" With TMG, you will be understood and heartfelt, with no concern about verbal language barriers.

INTERVENTIONAL MIND GESTALTATION

Differentiation of square versus circle, recognizing green versus red, and understanding $1 + 1 = 2$, for example, must have corresponding identifiable mind gestalts. Neurology already can assign many specific brain functions to specific neuron groups. Further studies may one day link specific feelings and thoughts to specific neuronal and mind gestalts.

Just like fingerprints and computerized facial features can identify persons, snapshots of mind gestalts may identify persons *by their minds.* Besides detecting lies, mind gestalt computing might enable direct reading of intentions and feelings. After all, some robots are already capable of "understanding" some human feelings. One day, they may come equipped with custom files of human mind gestalts that enable them to do so much more. There could be *robotic* pets. The legally blind could have a choice of high-tech seeing-eye dogs or pigs that understand human minds. Besides driving for you, friendly "auto" automobiles may try to soothe your anxiety when you are late for an important date.

In education, the analysis of mind gestalts may pinpoint areas of weakness in neuronal gestaltations and subject them to therapy. In simpler forms, electrocardiographic mapping already allows the treatment of atrial fibrillation by specific circuit disruption. Lobotomies and lobectomies of the brain have been used to treat selected psychiatric disorders. Relative to these surgical procedures, gestaltation therapy would be noninvasive, specific, direct, precise, and humane. Mental illnesses like schizophrenia may involve faulty links among sensory, cognitive, and affect gestalts, subject to therapeutic re-gestaltation. Mind gestalt training might alleviate autism. For a brief update on the advances in the neurotechnology of learning, see R. L. Hotz's "Brain Gains," the *Wall Street Journal*, August 13, 2021.

Pain, phobia, depression, and addiction are major sources of human suffering. Conceivably, mind gestalt intervention may offer relief. Since the ionic fluxes that constitute the electrophysiological potentials are downstream to the receptors, mind gestalt intervention bypasses all upstream issues related to neuronal transmitters and receptors. Such interventions may still work in the presence of transmitter deficiency, receptor desensitization, and other synaptic failures.

Personal Secrets and Privacy

The US Constitution guarantees freedom of thought, and the Fifth Amendment protects citizens' right to remain silent. In this aspect, analysis of the mind gestalts will have serious political and human-right implications. Mind gestalt analysis is, obviously, more invasive and extensive than lie detectors.

Uses and Abuses of Artificial Mind Gestaltation (AMG)

Besides making the blind see and the deaf hear, AMG can improve learning, memory, mental health, and well-being. Feelings can be shared by sharing files of mind gestalts. Tension and anxiety can be alleviated. Most importantly, pain can be relieved, and happiness can be achieved without chemicals. Drug addictions can be cured or prevented.

Demand for artificial happiness has been illustrated in the literature. King Giphad will be able to cure his son Jonash's sadness without the elusive "shirt of a happy man." All poor Prince Jonash needs is an AMG helmet loaded with a few good happiness files. Advanced AMG will be able to deliver ecstasies, laughter, sweet dreams, and tranquility directly to the cerebral neurons. With satiety files, obesity can be cured effortlessly, even happily.

At present, we relive our good experiences by recording and playing them back or by revisiting the physical gestalts. Physical gestalts, such as a loved one or a wedding, however, may no longer be there to be revisited. The storage of mind gestalts may one day become a reality. Recorded mind gestalts may enable realistic and enhanced reliving of treasured memory. After all, gramophones, tape recorders, eight-tracks, videotapes, and compact disks are obsolete, and DVDs are due for a major improvement. Artificial mind gestalt recording may be next. High-fidelity mind gestalt files of happiness can even be rented. Consumers would have a choice of genre of happiness. You can email a file of your feelings to friends; however, they may not care. Pleasant mind gestalts will likely be more welcome than boring complaints.

There are downsides to artificial mind gestaltation. Just two examples: One, it may itself be addictive, as all pleasurable experiences may; two, it will be open to abuses, such as brainwashing, dehumanization, instigation, and slavery. Drug lords may drive their victims to unlawful behaviors. In a way more direct and powerful than mass hypnosis, dictators and mob instigators may drive their followers wild. Once forced to wear an abusive AMG helmet, a victim may become a dehumanized living-slave robot. (See also "Wearable Mind-Controlling Headpieces" below.)

Tainan Lee 李清木

ANESTHESIA, SEDATION, THERAPEUTIC MIND GESTALTATION

Sedation is a component of anesthesia, commonly also used alone in intensive care and in lesser anesthesia for the likes of colonoscopy. Anesthesia is an intensive medical practice that renders patients surgically operable. It employs multiple drugs, techniques and monitors. The Bispectral index (BIS) is one monitor of the depth of anesthesia based on a Bispectral analysis of the surface brain waves. Therapies for mental illnesses include ECT (electric shock therapy). All these therapeutic interventions could one day be done by a new technique called "therapeutic mind gestaltation."

Whether subhuman animals and human fetuses and newborn babies have the capacity to suffer used to be a matter of debate. Notoriously, vivisectionists once used live animals for medical and physiological experiments without anesthesia or pain relief. As recently as the 1950s, physicians still debated whether fetuses and newborns have the mental capacity to suffer. Even when they provided anesthesia care to neonates, they were mainly concerned with cardiovascular instability, not pain and suffering. Since then, the secretion of stress hormones and other substances, along with cardiovascular responses, has been taken as indications that newborns and even fetuses can suffer. It would be interesting to medical sciences and humanity if mind gestalts of pain and suffering can be quantified and countered directly, irrespective of species and age. Buddhism asserts that all sentients can suffer and therefore deserve tender loving care. See "The Super-mind Gestalts" below.

Spinal Cord Electrophysiological Gestalt Therapy

Although not considered "mind," electrophysiological gestalts of the spinal cord play important roles in the life, feeling, happiness, and suffering of all vertebrates. Pain therapy has already taken spinal cord approaches with great success. Low back pain, incontinence, and erectile dysfunctions might one day be subjected to therapeutic electrophysiological re-gestaltation via the spinal cord.

Anecdotes

Telepathy and Telemind

If natural mind gestalts can be perceived by another brain directly, it would be telepathy. This is hard to do because emitted brain waves are weak, and we do not have the faculty to receive and decode them. Stage shows of telepathy are just entertainment because the entertainers utilize magic tricks and sneaky sensory inputs. Technology might one day enable computer transmission of real mind gestalts, just like radio transmits sound. This would be "telemind," so to speak. As long as the electromagnetic energy can excite the proper neurons, such mind files can be shared, even where there is no air and there are no visible lights.

A simple internet search of "牵魂" (literally "soul leading," pinyin *qianhun*) found items of 牵魂 and 牵亡魂, meaning "leading the soul of the deceased back to meet you." In 1955, my neighbor in the village vividly described her sentimental reunion with her deceased daughter, with the help of a soul leader. Although incredible and superstitious, some vivid descriptions of the "soul leading" scenes could be amazing and almost convincing. Rather than the soul of the deceased being led back to meet you, it could more likely be that the "leader" is using "telepathy" tricks to skillfully sense your deep feelings about the deceased and in turn talk to you "on behalf of" the deceased. The conversations could be very emotional and realistic. In most cases, the "leader" seems to have hypnotized himself just before the service, and the clients have been well preconditioned to focus on thoughts and feelings about the deceased. Furthermore, the "leader" and the clients must be close by, often in some physical contact, such as touching hands. Sometimes the leading attempts fail. It would be interesting if training could enhance a person's ability to sense the brain waves of another strongly preconditioned person.

CULTURE, LINGERING MELODIES, HAUNTING SMILES

Matter gestalts affect the mind gestalts not only individually but also as a culture. Daoism stresses the yin-yang harmony of natural gestalts, such as sun and moon, man and woman, fire and water, and weather and mood. Asian custom appreciates feng shui (風水), which is the gestalt energy derived from how things are arranged and how qi (氣, air, sound, and light) permeates the furniture, the buildings, the mountains, and the valleys. Temples are typically built on sites that have great feng shui. Interior designers gestaltate the furniture to harness good feng shui to induce mind gestalts that yield positive energy. You can sense good feng shui the moment you enter a room with it. Although not often referred to as such, good feng shui may attract customers and promote sales in stores.

Writers and philosophers like to muse about lingering gestalts. After a bird flies through the sky, Taoists wonder, "What 'footprints' does it leave behind?" Wandering scholar Laocan (老殘, 劉鶚) described the amazing haunting melody of Ms. Wangxiaoyu's (王小玉) storytelling as "lingering around the ceiling beams for more than three days" (餘音繞梁, 三日不絕). The sound gestalts of her verses must have dispersed soon after her chanting. However, the pleasant mind gestalts her sound excited in her fans' minds may linger for a long time. Physiologically, excited neuronal cell membranes have lowered thresholds and tend to fire action potentials again and again. Facilitated mind gestalts tend to repeat.

The traditional American folk song "*Her Bright Smiles Haunt Me Still*" is sung all over the world. The girl is gone, and we may never meet again; meanwhile "*I have struggled to forget, but the struggle was in vain.*" Imagine: "*Her voice lives on the breeze, and her spirit comes at will.*" Envision: "*In the midnight on the seas, her bright smiles haunt me still.*" In the 1950s, we sang this song in a Chinese version. The starting verse is "雲想衣裳花想容, Clouds reminiscent of her dresses, flowers reminiscent of her countenance." The poem was composed by the great poet Lee Pai (Li Bai, 李白) as a tribute to Lady Yang (楊貴妃), one of the Four Beauties in Chinese history and the heartily missed lover of Emperor Taizong of the Tang Dynasty (唐太宗), China. What a haunting beauty!

Mind gestalts are intrinsic to sentients, and humanity

transcends cultures. It is not rare for people to fall in love without the same spoken language. Loving mind gestalts can echo back and forth through great distances expeditiously and repetitively.

Wearable Mind-Controlling Headpieces
Controlling someone with a wearable device on the head is not a new idea. In the masterpiece *The Journey West* (西遊記), the almighty temperamental Monkey King (孫悟空) was controlled by his master, the Reverend Tang Monk (唐僧玄奘), with a cute-looking headpiece (the Tight Ring 緊箍圈). The headpiece would tighten every time the reverend invoked a secret incantation. Magically, it worked without electricity.

Figure: The fearless fighter Monkey King Sun WuKong was controllable only by a head ring that caused severe headache upon the recitation of a secret incantation by his master, the Reverend Tang Monk.

The Super-mind Gestalts

THE SENTIENCE AND THE "I" GESTALTS

Are there special super-mind gestalts that are the sentience gestalt (有情結搭), the "I" gestalt (自我結搭), or the soul gestalt (靈魂結搭)? All sentient animals sense and act sensibly. That is what enables earthworms to sense their surroundings and *sense up* which way to go for a better life. When cut, earthworms twist in a way that can be seen as suffering. Higher sentient species also have an "I" gestalt. Then comes also the "you" gestalt, as sentients evolved to differentiate "you and me." The sense of "others" followed. This evolution brought about all virtues and evils, as animals evolved to love, to hate, to fight, and to kill. The "I" gestalt is also the cause of all worries of the mortals.

Religions teach the harmony of the "I and others" gestalts. Taoism stresses the harmony of man and nature. Buddhism extends compassion to all sentients. Christianity preaches agape and God's love. Cogito or *sentio*, it is the "I" gestalt that realizes the "*sum*."

Tainan Lee 李清木

The Soul Gestalt

What sentient species on Earth are mindful enough to have soul, beyond and above sentience? One related biological question is: How many neurons will it take to hold a soul gestalt? Another question is: At what point does the soul enter the new body? One plausible answer would be that the soul enters the brain when a neuronal gestalt has grown capable to hold and to nurture it. Similar answers may apply to the sentience and the "I" gestalts of lower species not mindful enough to have a soul.

It is sometimes said that the departure of the soul from the body could take time, up to hours or days. For the purpose of organ donation, brain death is defined at a rather early stage of cessation of cortical functions. These medico-legal criteria could be at odds with religious beliefs. In practice, organ harvesting is performed under minimal anesthesia while maintaining a good heartbeat and blood circulation to assure the quality of the donated organs. When you are no longer "with it," *that's it!* One day, organs and tissues grown in vitro from donated samples may relieve the shortages of donated organs.

Could the soul reside anywhere other than the brain? The "I" gestalt mainly concerns the present life. It most likely resides in the brain cortex. The sentience, the soul, and karma concern also afterlives. Where they reside was historically a debate. Modern neurosciences and prevailing laws agree that they also reside in the brain, not in the heart or in the breath.

A Gestalt Theory of the Universe and the Mind

THE SENTIENT ID, THE KARMA, THE AFTERLIFE GESTALT
To be reincarnated fairly, life after life, karma bears detailed records of all prior deeds (業果), good and bad—not only deeds but thoughts too. Secret evil thoughts and bad words may be hidden from mothers and police, but nothing can be hidden or simply deleted from karma. Bad entries in karma can only be countered, furloughed, or ameliorated by payback, repentance, and dedicated blessings. You can help by praying for the needy soul.

A modus operandi is perhaps that each sentient has a core ID gestalt, akin to a "read and write" chip that identifies billions of individual citizens. The appropriate "I" gestalt, soul gestalt, and karma are then attached to the ID gestalt. The karma will be saved as an updated file at the end of each life. Before full enlightenment, all items in a sentient's karma book (業果簿) are not fully redeemed in each incarnation. Unrealized credits and debits are carried forward. Accordingly, each sentient will be bestowed a *ready and able* neuronal gestalt to serve each life. You will have appropriate mental and physical faculties to enjoy, and, sadly, also to bear and to suffer. Along this line of thought, the variable size of the afterlife gestalt likely modulates the range of cross-reincarnations among sentient species. It will therefore require most mortals many reincarnations to accumulate sufficient credits by gradual promotions (增上生) to attain nirvana. If it were not for reincarnation, you would have only one chance (during this short present life) to upgrade your eternal future, be it in hell or in heaven.

Reported on the internet are rare cases of children remembering their preceding lives. Conceivably, certain memories are accidentally appended to karma. This should be very rare because consequences of past lives are supposed to be "*sentienced*" (感果), not remembered or understood.

DEITIES AND OUR MIND GESTALTS

How do God, gods, and the omniscient hear our prayers, if not *mind to mind*? Vocal prayers, offerings, and symbols do not go far, but they help the praying mortals compose their mind gestalts.

We depict gods in our likeness—or rather, God created us in his likeness. However, bodies are for mortals only. Gods need no embodiment, and they need no sound waves to "hear" us. Being omnipresent, they have great sensitivity for devout prayers. Just like we have millions and millions of times more neurons than less developed sentients, gods could have trillions of times more powerful mind gestalts than we do. After all, a *Homo sapiens* has only about 1 kg of mushy brain to synthesize his mind gestalts. We are humble beings and should be.

Mind to mind, gods have no language barriers with us. They do not need verbal or written languages. Even among mortals, similar feelings are often expressed in similar mind gestalts, irrespective of language preferences. Some mortals even have the sixth sense.

A Gestalt Theory of the Universe and the Mind

GESTALTS IN THE SPACE-TIME WEB

If after death I go to heaven or to reincarnation, what goes on my behalf? Whatever that may be, how does it rise above the decaying neurons *whole*, to travel the Sea of Strands *intact*? Reincarnation further raises questions of fairness and accuracy, such as "How does the good karma that I deserve stay with me?" We mortals have no answers to these questions. Neither do we know how eternal life and deities live forever without embodiment and without neurons. According to this gestalt model, all super-mind gestalts are *durable* mind gestalts of electromagnetic energy.

As the fabric of the Universe and vehicle of transport of electromagnetic energy, the ubiquitous Sea of Strands likely transmits our prayers. It likely also transports our souls after our death. Nothing else can do it. As electromagnetic energy, all mind gestalts should travel by the Sea of Strands. God willing, his will also descends upon us via the Space-Time Web. As illustrated by Newton's cradle, the strands are the ultimate relayers of electromagnetic energy, including all mind and super-mind gestalts. The Sea of Strands relays electromagnetic energy *in all directions at all times*, economic in energy and efficient in performance.

Imagine space-time as a four-dimensional super-web of lively strands. *We are all together and connected!* Here and there, sentients and mortals live in their worlds. Salvaged souls live in their heavens. Deities reside in and rule from their holy kingdoms. Unsettled souls wait in limbo. Ghosts loiter around. Hells have their places in the Space-Time Web too. Via the web, the omniscient hear our prayers. Via the web, we also feel their presence, their will and their power, especially when we pray for "Thy kingdom come!" Beyond the reach of light and sound, merciful deity Bodhisattva Guanyin (觀音菩薩) likely senses the perturbations of the Space-Time Web when suffering sentients ask for mercy.

(NB: These thoughts on the super-mind gestalts extend solely from my gestalt theory. They do not represent my religion, nor the teachings of the learned in religions. They are intended for a casual discussion and have no asserted veracity. Readers with questions should follow their own beliefs and consult higher advisers.)

摘要 (Abstract in Traditional Chinese)

一：陰陽結搭宇宙說

無中生有，物理學說不可能。但是宇宙必須出之於無，不然，它的先驅必定又有其先驅，終究來自虛無。在太虛（the Void），本來無物、無間、無時。無中如何生有？首先初陰（yin 1，陰1）出現，並在「無時」之內引導出初陽（yang 1，陽1），使陰陽結搭（gestalt，全形）歸零。這初陰初陽，絕對微小，有互補引力（gravity）、有微能。既以「異時微動」而逃避兩相殲滅，又以同樣「歸零互生」法，陰1引生（induce）陽2，陽1也引生陰2。從此，每個陰陽子都以無限速度引生異性微子。每個陰陽子，每一代，子子孫孫連串又分叉，以幾何級數無限增生。既然步步歸零，不用輸入能源，就不受限制，因此宇宙的前身（pre-Universe）就增生成無限緊密的原球（the Ball）。原球終於變成無限擠塞，一旦飽和或有所不勻，必定爆炸（Big Bang，the Bang，大爆），粉碎分散成縷（strands）。縷含有陰陽串，陰端，和陽端。其陰端、

Tainan Lee 李清木

陽端各有微能，也互有引力，不斷結搭。從此，宇宙存在。宇宙始於一物一時空（一物，縷；一時空，distance-time），終成萬物，有度量衡、時空（space-time）和物理。縷相互結搭而成質能，量子，光子，原子、星系、銀河等等。縷海是宇宙的支架，包含全宇宙，也是電磁能傳遞的媒介。今日宇宙，萬物無限互動，然而全宇宙依舊維持陰陽平衡，總體歸零。佛教心經說「色即是空，空即是色」。「不生不滅」、「不增不減」。故，悟空即悟實。宇宙一切都是陰陽結搭 (yin-yang gestalt)，由虛無以結搭而成實體。電子和原子核，非結搭不成原子。量子，地球，以致星系依復如是，似有非有，非有而有，都是活動結搭。質是相對穩定的穩態結搭，能是相對不穩定的暫態結搭。結搭本是無常的動相。故，宇宙無常。陰陽縷所結搭而成的宇宙本無直線，無平面，無正圓，不對稱。光子也是縷的結搭，放射後順時空（space-time）在引力的牽制下，螺旋前進。太虛無地址，一切都是相對的。時、空、質能、度量衡、思維都是暫時的。萬物、人性、知識、智慧與靈性，憑心靈結搭來領悟而成真。宇宙會不會消滅？如果陰子和陽子正面相向、擠入同一時空，兩者會同歸於盡。接著陰陽串也可能連鎖消失。這消失的可能性與連鎖消失的程度不堪揣測。如果連鎖消失後，宇宙只剩下單單一個陰子或陽子，如 yin 1似的無拘無束，宇宙可能再生。

二：結搭心靈說

萬物皆空，一切都以結搭而存在。我們的思維也是結搭。腦細胞以其細胞突觸（ｓｙｎａｐｓｅｓ）產生突觸作用電勢

（synaptic action potentials）再結搭而型成心靈結搭（mind gestalts）。突觸結搭是有形結搭，相對穩定。電勢結搭，是暫態結搭，相對不穩定，一現即散。心靈結搭演變成一切有情眾生的感覺、感受、思考、智能與智慧。眾生有情，以心靈結搭來與外界事物互感互動。隨物種進化，腦神經細胞增多，腦細胞的排列與細胞突觸的結搭越加複雜、高明。人類的中樞神經有千億(10^{11})腦細胞，極多的突觸，更多的突觸作用電勢。每一個突觸作用電勢又是極多的鈉鉀等離子的進出流動所致。這些作用電勢，結搭而使一切有情眾生（sentients）有感覺，有自我感，有身心活動，也有感受、感情、思維、理智、智慧（統稱心靈）。「我思故我在」（ Cogito, ergo sum ），「思」是腦細胞在探索，「在」是自我意識（ sum gestalt ）。宇宙萬物，既以結搭而無中生有，有情眾生，又以心靈結搭而識別自我和萬物，故，筆者曰：「我識故我在, Sentio, ergo sum!」宇宙以縷海成型，電磁能依縷海傳遞，時空如蛛網，在時空網(Space-Time Web)人畜、鬼神、天國、地獄個有所處，互依互動。有一天，憑電腦科技和人工智能，人類可能將心靈結搭加以分析、改進，進而分享感受和智慧，甚至修改病態、造福一切眾生。

About the Author and the Book

by Ytenne Lee

Professor Chingmuh Lee, 李清木, was born in Taiwan. He was interested in a physics major but was persuaded to study medicine. In medicine, he pursued anesthesiology research and made a tenured professorship at age thirty-nine. Besides his main  profession, Dr. Lee pursued multiple interests, including hiking, music, and fantasizing about the Universe.

Dr. Lee has a medical degree from the National Taiwan University, an anesthesiology specialty residency from the University of Pittsburgh, and an anesthesiology research fellowship from Harvard Medical School. He held faculty positions at Duke University and at

Tainan Lee 李清木

UCLA. In his academic career, Dr. Lee published profusely in peer-reviewed publications and has lectured widely on the basic and clinical sciences of neuromuscular pharmacology.

This book, although profound and creative in theory, is written for easy reading in order to satisfy a common human desire to "grasp" the unfathomable Universe and the amazing human mind. It is based on popular sciences made easy. Background information can easily be found in public domains on the internet.

Many of us enjoy fantasizing about the Universe. How did it happen, what is the Big Bang, and where are we? We also wonder about our mind. Is it real? This book provides a fun theory for readers to think along. The story begins with a tiny yin balanced by a tiny yang, neither recognizable as a *being* alone. However, their unstoppable zero-sum chain multiplication resulted in the Big Ball that exploded into strands at the Big Bang. The strands then form the Sea of Strands and make particles, atoms, stars, and galaxies by gestaltation. Gestaltation also makes up the mind.

The Universe as a whole has a zero-sum. However, everything is real as a gestalt. The nucleus and the electrons are not the atom; their gestalt is the atom. The story gets even more exciting when you try to grasp the galaxies, the mind, and the deities.

Think along. You will be immersed, challenged, and entertained.

A Gestalt Theory of the Universe and the Mind

ABOUT YTENNE LEE

Ytenne Lee is an American board-certified anesthesiologist with a master's degree in public health from Harvard. He is also a math aficionado and a self-taught computer programmer. His mathematical works include a formula to solve quintic equations, finding the last three nonzero digits of (90!), and the unwrapping of a conic section. His computer programs include one to solve Rubik's cubes and one to calculate the winning probabilities of poker hands. The author is grateful to Ytenne for the first reading of the manuscript and for his contribution to the back cover of the book.

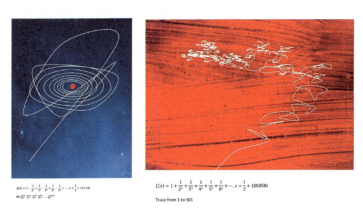

Figure: Ytenne's mathematical artworks, with formulas. *First Convergence*, left; *A Spring Hike to the Cherry Blossom Garden in the Space-Time Web*, right.

Made in the USA
Columbia, SC
23 August 2022